© Stonewell Healing Press, 2025
All rights reserved.

This book is a labor of care. Please do not copy, share, or distribute any part of it—digitally or physically—without written permission from the author or publisher, except for brief excerpts used in reviews or critical articles. Your respect helps this work reach others who need it.

This workbook is not a replacement for therapy, crisis support, or mental health treatment. It's meant to offer reflection, comfort, and growth—not clinical care. If you're struggling, please reach out to a licensed professional. You matter too much to go through it alone.

Every effort has been made to ensure this content is accurate, responsible, and thoughtful. The author and publisher cannot guarantee outcomes and are not liable for misuse or misinterpretation of the material.

Thank you for being here. We're honored to walk beside you.

M. Tourangeau
Stonewell Healing Press

TABLE OF CONTENTS

SECTION 1 -   1

Recognizing Emotional Abuse in Co-Parenting – When It's Not Just 'Over'

SECTION 2-   31

Understanding the Trauma Bond Without Romance – Why You're Still Hooked

SECTION 3 -   61

Setting Boundaries When 'No Contact' Isn't an Option

SECTION 4 -   93

The Guilt, Shame, and Self-Doubt of Parenting Through Abuse

SECTION 5-   127

Managing Emotional Hijacks: Regulating Yourself When Triggered

SECTION 6   157

Navigating Conflict Without Losing Yourself

Stonewell Healing Press

TABLE OF CONTENTS

SECTION 7 -   **191**

When Co-Parenting Triggers Old Wounds – Healing Your Inner Child

---

SECTION 8-   **217**

Healing the Trauma Bond – Breaking Free Within Co-Parenting

SECTION 9 -   **245**

Self-Forgiveness & Untangling the Shame Spiral

SECTION 10 -   **275**

Relearning Love – What Healthy Relationships Actually Feel Like

---

SECTION 11 -   **301**

Future You – Trusting Yourself Again

CLOSING   **331**

Stonewell Healing Press

Dedicated to the parents who are forcing calm into rooms filled with chaos, just so their kids could feel a moment of peace.

STONEWELL HEALING PRESS

HOW TO USE THIS WORKBOOK

Take your time with this. The more you pause to really think about each question and answer honestly, the more space you create for reflection. And with deeper reflection, this experience can open up new understanding and healing you might not expect.

Be honest with yourself—there's no judgment here. This is your private space. If you want, you can even throw this book away or burn it later to keep your secrets safe. That said, be mindful of how much you dive in. Healing and reflection around tough, sensitive topics can bring up strong feelings—and yes, it can get triggering. So here's your gentle trigger warning.

The real progress comes when you practice the skills, not just read about them. The more you try them out in your life, the more helpful this workbook will be.

STONEWELL HEALING PRESS

ASSESSMENT

WHERE AM I NOW?

Before we begin, take a moment to honestly check in with yourself by rating these statements on a scale from 1 (not at all) to 10 (completely):

1. I feel emotionally safe during exchanges or communication with my co-parent.

2. I can set and keep boundaries without guilt or second-guessing.

3. I trust my own perception of events, even when my co-parent denies or twists them.

4. I no longer feel responsible for managing my co-parent's emotions.

5. I can disengage from baiting or manipulation without losing my calm.

6. I have effective ways to regulate my body and mind after tense interactions.

7. I prioritize my own mental health and my child's well-being over pleasing my co-parent.

8. I believe I can create a stable, nurturing environment for my child despite my co-parent's behavior.

SECTION ONE

Recognizing Emotional Abuse in Co-Parenting — When It's Not Just 'Over'

Surviving emotional abuse isn't always about leaving a romantic relationship and walking away. Sometimes, it's about surviving the ongoing pain and manipulation that comes with co-parenting an emotional abuser — a person who may no longer be your partner, but who still has the power to hurt, control, and unsettle your life. This isn't your typical break-up story. It's about navigating a complicated, messy, and often exhausting dynamic where love might have died, but trauma lives on.

In this section, you'll begin to recognize what emotional abuse looks like in co-parenting — the covert control, the gaslighting, the guilt-trips disguised as concern. You'll learn why this abuse can feel so confusing and why your feelings are valid. You're not alone, and the exhaustion and overwhelm you feel make complete sense. Together, we'll lay the foundation for understanding this unique kind of abuse and how it shows up in your life.

Making Sense Of It
The Trap of Co-Parenting with an Abuser

Co-parenting with an emotional abuser is one of the most disorienting experiences a parent can face. The romantic relationship may have ended, but the tactics of control rarely stop — they simply shift form. What was once jealousy, criticism, or gaslighting in private may now show up as "co-parenting disagreements," subtle guilt trips, or manipulative claims made in the name of what's "best for the child." The breakup doesn't grant you freedom; it often reshapes the abuse into a new, court-sanctioned container.

From a psychological lens, this is deeply complex because it traps you in what researchers call a prolonged trauma bond — a pattern where your nervous system stays tethered to the person who harmed you. Fear, guilt, and hope get tangled together, leaving you hyper-attuned to their moods and reactions. And unlike many survivors who can choose "no contact," you are compelled to maintain regular interaction, because your child becomes the bridge you both must cross.

Anthropologically, parenthood has always been tied to survival — children link families, clans, and communities. That evolutionary weight means that when your co-parent undermines you, it's not just personal — it strikes at something primal: your role as protector and provider. No wonder your body reacts with tension, exhaustion, or dread after each exchange. It isn't overreaction. It's your nervous system preparing for danger.

The first step toward healing is naming the truth: you are not failing, you are enduring. The fatigue, self-doubt, and emotional whiplash you feel are not weakness — they are evidence of how heavy this reality truly is. Recognizing this allows you to release some of the self-blame and begin building strategies that protect both you and your child from the ongoing cycle of manipulation.

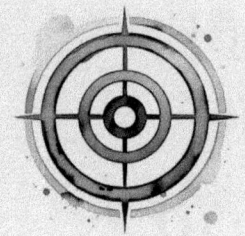

Trigger Check-In

You're waiting at the school gate for your child's pickup. Your ex arrives late, avoids eye contact, and slips your child into your arms without a word. Then, as you turn to leave, a casual comment about "how you handle your parenting" cuts sharp and cold, leaving you second-guessing yourself all the way home. You try to shrug it off, but that knot in your stomach tightens. The exhaustion isn't just physical — it's emotional and lingering.

I see you holding your breath in moments like these. I see how exhausting it is to walk this tightrope, balancing your child's needs with your own emotional safety. Your feelings are real and valid. It's okay to feel tired, confused, and unsure — these are the natural effects of surviving abuse that didn't end when the relationship did.

What does emotional abuse look like in my co-parenting experience?

Reflect on specific behaviors or patterns that feel controlling, manipulative, or draining. Naming these can bring clarity.

What does emotional abuse look like in my co-parenting experience?

How has ongoing contact affected my emotional and physical well-being?

Explore the toll of constant interaction with your co-parent. What sensations or feelings arise?

How has ongoing contact affected my emotional and physical well-being?

In what ways might I still be trauma bonded to my co-parent?

Consider moments when you feel stuck, hopeful, or fearful around them.

In what ways might I still be trauma bonded to my co-parent?

How does my child's presence impact my feelings about this relationship?

Reflect on how your child connects you to your co-parent, both emotionally and practically.

How does my child's presence impact my feelings about this relationship?

What beliefs or messages about myself have I absorbed through this co-parenting abuse?

Identify any self-doubt, guilt, or blame you carry.

What beliefs or messages about myself have I absorbed through this co-parenting abuse?

When have I noticed my nervous system reacting during or after interactions?

Describe sensations, emotional states, or physical symptoms.

When have I noticed my nervous system reacting during or after interactions?

What would it feel like to start setting emotional boundaries in this ongoing relationship?

Visualize what safety and control might look like.

What would it feel like to start setting emotional boundaries in this ongoing relationship?

What small act of self-compassion can I offer myself today related to co-parenting struggles?

List concrete ways to nurture your emotional health, even in tiny moments.

What small act of self-compassion can I offer myself today related to co-parenting struggles?

TRACING THE TRUTH

EMOTION MAPPING CHART

When co-parenting with someone abusive, it's easy to get pulled into overthinking. Every text or action can feel like proof of a bigger agenda. This exercise helps you separate what actually happened from the story your mind builds around it — giving you more clarity and less emotional exhaustion.

Why it helps:
Abuse thrives on confusion. When you can clearly see the difference between what happened and the story you tell about it, you interrupt the cycle of self-doubt and emotional hijacking. This practice restores some of your power — because you can't always change your co-parent's behavior, but you can reclaim how you make sense of it.

In the "Facts" column, list only what you know for certain — direct actions, words, or agreements. Keep it objective (e.g., "We exchange at 6pm," "She texted me three times yesterday").

In the "Stories" column, write the meanings or assumptions you add (e.g., "He's trying to ruin my evening," "She doesn't respect me").

Ask yourself three questions:
Is this story fully true, or partly interpretation?
Is there another possible explanation?
Does this story help me co-parent — or make it harder?

Circle What's Useful
Put a circle around the stories that strengthen you or keep you steady, and cross out the ones that drain your energy or increase conflict.

TRACING THE TRUTH

EMOTION MAPPING CHART

FACTS **STORIES**

TRACING THE TRUTH

EMOTION MAPPING CHART

FACTS	STORIES

CHECKPOINT

What If I Relapse?

It's okay if, despite your best efforts, you find yourself slipping into old patterns — doubting yourself, reacting emotionally, or feeling overwhelmed. These setbacks don't erase your progress. When this happens:
Pause and breathe deeply.
Use your grounding or reframing tools.
Reach out to a trusted friend or support.
Write a compassionate note to yourself.
You're learning new ways to survive and thrive in a difficult, ongoing situation. Patience and kindness toward yourself are essential.

EXTERNALIZE THE INNER CRITIC

The inner critic often masquerades as truth, when really it's a protective part gone overboard. By externalizing it — drawing it, collaging it, or writing it as a character — you create distance. Suddenly, it's not you failing; it's a scared or rigid part doing its job too harshly. Research in IFS and narrative therapy shows that putting dialogue on paper softens shame and restores self-leadership. Adding a Wise Friend voice gives you access to compassion and balance. The final boundary statement reminds the critic: its role is protection, not punishment. That's where healing starts.

Create the Critic — Draw, doodle, or collage how your inner critic might look. Don't worry about artistic skill.

Dialogue — Write a short back-and-forth:
You: "I hear you saying I'll fail."
Critic: "I don't want you to get hurt."
Wise Friend: "You can protect without tearing down."

Set a Boundary — End the dialogue with a firm line: "Your job is protection, not punishment. I'll take it from here."

MAPPING YOUR RESILIENCE

When life is painful, the spotlight lands on what's broken or lost. But every hard season you've lived through also carries evidence of your resilience. Mapping your past with a "strength lens" helps you reclaim those forgotten skills — endurance, creativity, boundary-setting, persistence, humor, or compassion. Trauma research shows that naming and revisiting these strengths rebuilds self-trust. Instead of seeing your past only as a string of wounds, you begin to recognize the ways you showed up for yourself. Circling three core strengths creates a personal toolkit you can consciously bring forward into your next chapter.

1. **Draw Your Timeline** —Mark a few "hard seasons" you've lived through on the timeline.

2. **Name Strengths** — Under each event, write one or two strengths you used to get through (e.g., courage, asking for help, persistence).

3. **Circle Three** — Look at the whole map. Circle three strengths that feel most alive, relevant, or needed for where you're headed now.

4. **Carry Them Forward** — Write them on a sticky note or card where you'll see them often — reminders that you've done hard things before, and you will again.

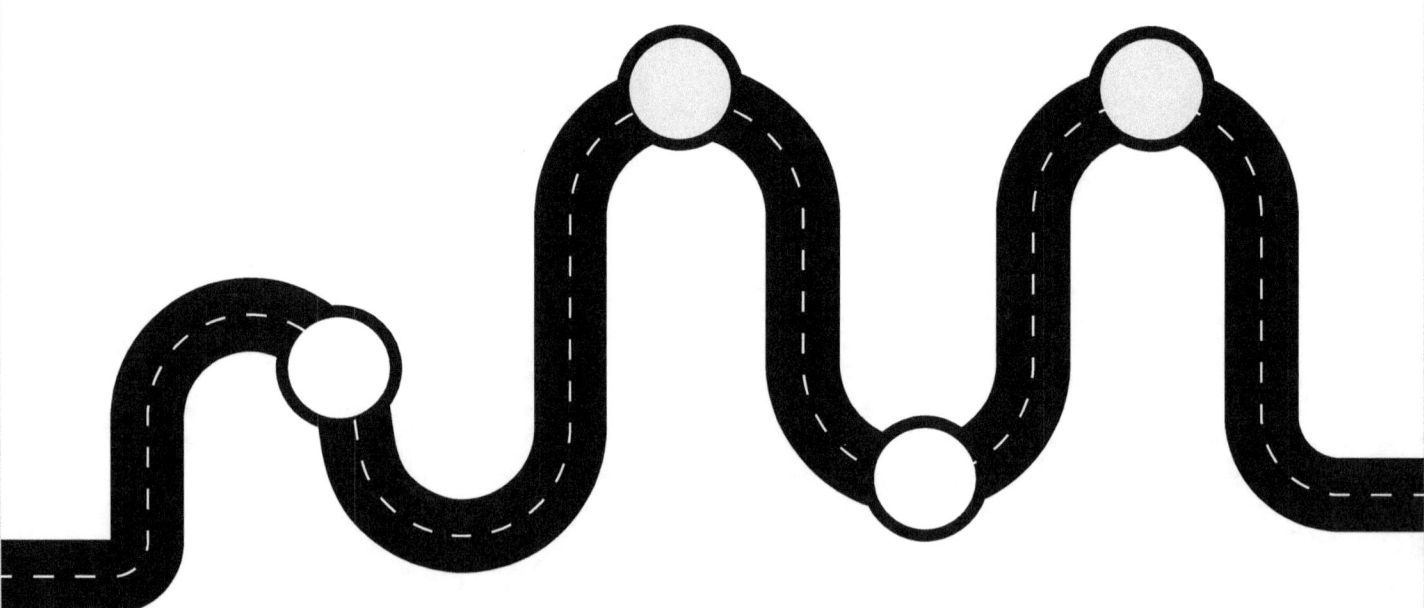

Letters To Your Future Self

Write a letter from your future self, who has learned to navigate co-parenting with strength and calm. What does that future you say about the journey you're on now? What hopes or advice would they share?

Letters To Your Future Self

Letters To Your Future Self

SECTION TWO

Understanding the Trauma Bond Without Romance — Why You're Still Hooked

When the romantic relationship ends, many expect the emotional pain to fade — but with an emotionally abusive co-parent, the pain often lingers, tangled up in your shared parenting responsibilities. You might wonder, "Why can't I just let go? Why do I feel so stuck?" This is the trauma bond at work — a confusing, powerful attachment born from cycles of harm and care, fear and hope.

In this section, you'll learn how trauma bonds evolve outside of romantic love, especially when your child connects you to your abuser. Understanding how your nervous system stays triggered by reminders of the past and by ongoing contact is key to breaking free. You're not trapped because you're weak or needy; you're responding to deep, survival-based wiring. Recognizing this truth is the foundation for healing and reclaiming your freedom.

Making Sense Of It Steadying the Storm: How You Become the Safe Place

One of the hardest truths about co-parenting with an addict is that you can't control the chaos your child witnesses. Children notice broken promises, last-minute cancellations, and mood swings. They feel disappointment and confusion, even if they don't say it out loud. Your role becomes the anchor: the one who offers consistent meals, bedtime routines, truthful explanations, and reassurance that they are safe and loved.

Protecting your child takes an enormous toll. You may carry extra financial burdens when the other parent doesn't pay what they should. You may sacrifice sleep, social life, or personal projects to maintain a sense of normalcy. Your body might ache from tension or exhaustion. Your heart carries guilt, fear, and rage, often all at once. Feeling these is normal—they are signs of deep care and high stakes.

Protection doesn't mean erasing all harm. It means creating small, steady islands of safety your child can rely on. Naming these moments—like reading together at night, explaining honestly why plans fell through, or keeping promises you can keep—teaches your child that stability is possible even in chaos. And crucially, this insight extends to you: your boundaries, self-care, and resilience are part of that protection. You are not just surviving this chaos—you are giving your child something they will carry with them long after these struggles pass.

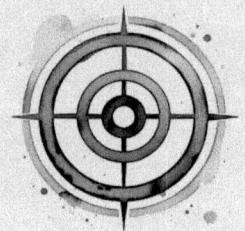 # Trigger Check-In

It's the morning after a tense custody exchange. You wake up feeling heavy, replaying every word and glance from yesterday. Your heart races, your mind spirals with "What if I'd said this differently?" The exhaustion seeps deep, but despite wanting distance, you catch yourself checking your phone for a message from your co-parent. That tug pulls you back into the cycle, even though you know it's painful.

I see you caught between wanting peace and feeling pulled back into the storm. I see how confusing it is to love your child fiercely while feeling trapped by the trauma bond. Your reactions make sense — they're part of your survival, not a failing. You're doing your best in an impossible situation.

What feelings come up when I notice myself still emotionally tied to my co-parent?

Explore the mix of hope, fear, anger, or sadness that keeps you connected.

What feelings come up when I notice myself still emotionally tied to my co-parent?

How does my nervous system react to different types of contact or reminders?

Describe physical sensations and emotional responses.

How does my nervous system react to different types of contact or reminders?

When have I noticed the cycle of tension and relief that characterizes my trauma bond?

Recall specific moments or patterns.

When have I noticed the cycle of tension and relief that characterizes my trauma bond?

In what ways do I hold onto the relationship for my child's sake?

Reflect on the complexities of love and responsibility.

In what ways do I hold onto the relationship for my child's sake?

What are some beliefs I have about myself that this trauma bond reinforces?

Identify any thoughts that may keep you stuck.

What are some beliefs I have about myself that this trauma bond reinforces?

How do I currently try to cope or break free from this emotional pull?

Note strategies you use, even if they aren't always effective.

How do I currently try to cope or break free from this emotional pull?

What would it look like to create emotional space for myself while still co-parenting?

Imagine boundaries and safety for your feelings.

What would it look like to create emotional space for myself while still co-parenting?

How can I show myself compassion as I navigate this ongoing bond?

List ways to nurture yourself gently and patiently.

How can I show myself compassion as I navigate this ongoing bond?

TRACING THE TRUTH

THE INVISIBLE LEDGER

When you carry so much responsibility, it's easy to minimize what it costs you—and what it gives your child. This reflection balances both truths.

Why it helps:
This exercise validates your exhaustion while also honoring the gift you're giving your child. Seeing both costs and gifts written down prevents you from minimizing your role or dismissing your efforts. It reframes your sacrifices as proof of your resilience and love.

In the first section, *"What This Has Cost Me"*, list the personal tolls you've felt from co-parenting with someone struggling with addiction. Examples might include sleepless nights, carrying extra bills, or the emotional strain of constant uncertainty. Be honest, even with the "small" costs—they all add up.

In the second section, *"What This Has Given My Child"*, list what your efforts have given your child, even indirectly. This might be a stable bedtime routine, the comfort of your reliability, or learning that love can be consistent.

Once you've filled both lists, pause and read them side by side. Notice how one exists because of the other—you've turned personal sacrifice into your child's sense of safety.

TRACING THE TRUTH

THE INVISIBLE LEDGER

What This Has Cost Me

What This Has Given My Child

TRACING THE TRUTH

ISLANDS OF SAFETY

When chaos feels constant, it's easy to forget the moments of protection and stability you are creating. Writing them down helps you recognize your strength and show yourself the credit you rarely give.

Why it helps:
Writing these side by side shows you what's often invisible: you can't erase the chaos, but you are giving your child islands of safety. Seeing this on paper reinforces your strength and steadiness.

In the first column: "The Chaos They Witnessed" write down specific examples of situations where the other parent's addiction caused instability—missed visits, unpredictable moods, broken promises. Be concrete and brief.
In the second column: "The Anchor I Provided" write what you did to steady your child in that moment. This might be as simple as keeping a routine, offering comfort, or telling the truth in age-appropriate words.
Aim for multiple examples so you can see the pattern of how often you've been the consistent one.

TRACING THE TRUTH

ISLANDS OF SAFETY

The Chaos They Witnessed

The Anchor I Provided

CHECKPOINT

Obsessing Over The Everyday

If you find yourself obsessing over your co-parent, checking messages repeatedly, or feeling emotionally hijacked, remember: This is part of the trauma bond cycle, not a personal failure. Try to pause, use your breathwork or grounding, and remind yourself of your values and goals. Reach out to your support system or write a compassionate note to yourself. Progress isn't linear, and each step forward counts.

MASK WORK

We all carry layers — the parts we show and the parts we protect. Trauma, stress, or social expectation often make us overinvest in the "front" mask while ignoring the care the "back" side needs. This exercise gives you a safe way to explore both sides without forcing exposure. By naming what's hidden, you acknowledge your needs; by sharing a small sliver with a trusted person, you practice vulnerability and connection without danger. It helps build trust in yourself — that you can both protect and reveal, and that your inner life is valid and worthy of care. Over time, you may notice your outer mask feels lighter, more authentic, because your inner self has space to be seen.

Fill Them In — List words, phrases, or images for each side. Don't censor yourself.

Choose a Safe Reveal — Pick one tiny sliver from the Back mask and plan to share it with a safe person this week.

Reflect — Notice what it feels like to acknowledge and/or reveal that part of yourself.

What the world sees | What you protect or that needs care

FEELING IN MOTION

Our bodies carry what words often can't — tension, joy, grief, or relief. Moving intentionally helps you process and release emotions stored in the body, while giving a tangible sense of your day's narrative. Ending in a posture of strength signals to your nervous system: I survived, I'm here, I can hold myself steady. This isn't about dancing perfectly or performing for anyone; it's about giving your inner experience a voice through movement, noticing how small gestures can express complex feelings. Over time, this practice reconnects body and mind, helping you feel grounded, seen, and resilient.

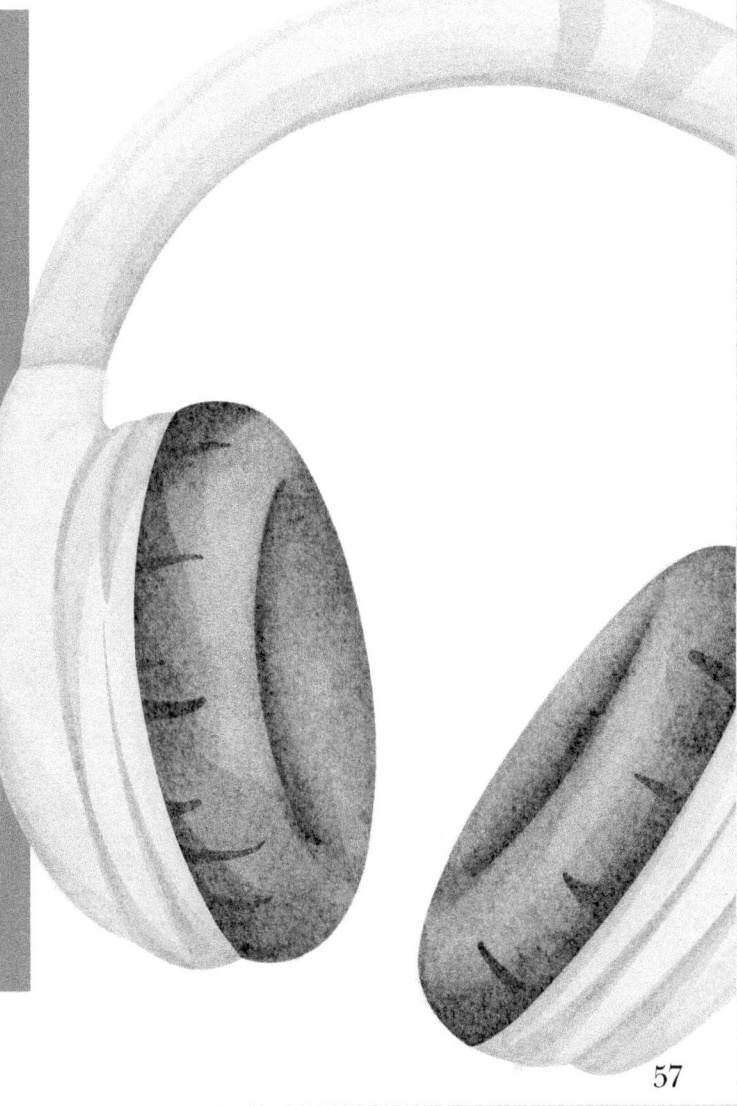

Choose a Song — Something that matches or invites movement for your current state.

Move Freely — Let your body express today's story. Small gestures count — a hand to heart, a sway, a shrug.

Notice — Pay attention to tension, ease, or areas that want attention.

End in Strength — Finish in a posture that conveys groundedness and safety (feet planted, shoulders relaxed, chest open). Hold for 30 seconds.

Reflect — Journal a few words about what your body expressed and how it feels afterward.

Letters To Your Future Self

Write a letter from your future self who has gently loosened the trauma bond. What wisdom and encouragement does that future you offer about this journey?

Letters To Your Future Self

SECTION THREE

Setting Boundaries When 'No Contact' Isn't an Option

In most recovery journeys, "no contact" is the golden rule — a boundary that protects your healing by cutting off abusive interactions. But when you're co-parenting an emotional abuser, "no contact" is rarely an option. Your child is the bridge between you, and communication must happen — sometimes daily, sometimes unexpectedly. This makes boundary setting more complex, more urgent, and often more frustrating.

This section is your blueprint for creating strong, trauma-informed boundaries in a context where you cannot simply walk away. You'll learn practical strategies to protect your emotional space while fulfilling your parenting responsibilities. These boundaries aren't about punishment or confrontation — they're about preserving your peace, regulating your nervous system, and staying centered amid chaos. You will also receive carefully crafted "How to Respond" scripts for real-world communication, plus tools to prepare and recover emotionally from interactions that might trigger you. With these tools, you can reclaim control — not over your co-parent, but over your reactions, your energy, and your life.

Making Sense Of It
Boundaries as Survival Maps

Boundaries are not just rules you set with words — they're survival maps that guide your nervous system toward safety. In healthy relationships, boundaries create mutual respect and rhythm. But in the context of co-parenting with an emotionally abusive ex, boundaries often feel like sandcastles against the tide. The other parent may test, erode, or bulldoze them altogether, not because your boundaries are wrong, but because control is the currency of abuse.

From a psychological lens, your body reads every crossed boundary as a potential threat. Even a seemingly "small" violation — like ignoring an agreed pick-up time or sending hostile texts — can trigger fight, flight, or freeze, because your nervous system has learned that unpredictability signals danger. Anthropologically, this struggle mirrors survival in hostile environments: human groups have always used boundaries — from physical walls to social norms — to protect vulnerable members. When those are breached, the group must adapt quickly to stay safe. You are enacting that same ancient instinct, protecting your child and yourself in the face of instability.

What makes boundaries in this context so complex is that you can't disengage fully. Unlike typical abusive relationships where no-contact offers relief, co-parenting forces ongoing exposure. That's why internal boundaries matter just as much as external ones: the discipline of not answering every provocation, not absorbing every insult, not letting their chaos define your reality. External strategies (like written communication only, legal structures, or parallel parenting) combine with internal strategies (like regulating your breath before replying, reality-checking manipulations, and naming what is yours versus what is theirs).

Boundaries here are not about building walls of stone; they're about weaving flexible but strong nets. Nets that let the chaos pass through while still holding what matters most — your child's safety and your emotional equilibrium.

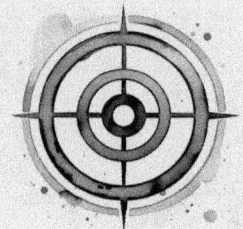 # Trigger Check-In

You receive a text late at night about a change in your child's schedule. It's vague and laced with a passive-aggressive tone that makes your chest tighten. You want to respond immediately, but you remember the boundary you've set: no emotional engagement after 8 PM. You breathe, pull out your phone, and send a calm, clear message: "Thanks for letting me know. I'll adjust accordingly." You put your phone down and go for a grounding walk before bed.

I see you juggling the impossible — wanting to protect your child, maintain peace, and keep your own heart whole. I see how exhausting it is to face the daily micro-battles of communication, the constant testing of your boundaries. You are stronger than you realize, and every step you take to protect your space is a victory.

What boundaries have I tried to set with my co-parent, and how were they respected or violated?

Reflect on successes and challenges to understand your current patterns.

What boundaries have I tried to set with my co-parent, and how were they respected or violated?

How do I feel physically and emotionally before, during, and after interactions with my co-parent?

Notice sensations and emotional shifts to spot early warning signs.

How do I feel physically and emotionally before, during, and after interactions with my co-parent?

What communication methods (text, email, in-person) feel safest and most manageable for me?

Explore which channels help maintain your boundaries.

What communication methods (text, email, in-person) feel safest and most manageable for me?

What are my non-negotiable boundaries related to co-parenting communication?

List your essential limits, such as time of day, tone, or topic boundaries.

What are my non-negotiable boundaries related to co-parenting communication?

How can I prepare myself emotionally before planned communication?

Brainstorm rituals or practices that ground and steady you.

How can I prepare myself emotionally before planned communication?

When my boundaries are challenged, what are my most common emotional reactions?

Identify patterns like anger, freeze, or guilt.

When my boundaries are challenged, what are my most common emotional reactions?

How might I respond calmly and assertively when my co-parent crosses a boundary?

Visualize or write sample responses that feel authentic and safe.

How might I respond calmly and assertively when my co-parent crosses a boundary?

What support systems can I lean on when I feel overwhelmed by boundary challenges?

List people, groups, or self-care tools that help you reset.

What support systems can I lean on when I feel overwhelmed by boundary challenges?

TRACING THE TRUTH

INTERNAL VS. EXTERNAL BOUNDARIES

Boundaries aren't just about what you tell others — they're also about how you manage your inner responses. Strengthening internal boundaries helps prevent manipulation from hijacking your emotions.

Why it helps:
By connecting external rules with internal regulation, you train your nervous system to stay calm and centered even when abuse or chaos appears. This reduces reactive patterns, protects your energy, and reinforces your sense of control over your emotional space.

Under External Boundary, list one action you enforce with your co-parent (e.g., "I only respond to texts between 9–5").
Under Internal Boundary Response, write how you will manage your reaction if the external boundary is tested (e.g., "Pause, take three breaths, remind myself this is their chaos, not my failure").
Repeat for 5–8 scenarios you frequently face.
Circle one internal boundary you want to practice consciously this week.

TRACING THE TRUTH

INTERNAL VS. EXTERNAL BOUNDARIES

External Boundary　　　　　　　　**Internal Boundary**

TRACING THE TRUTH

MAPPING YOUR BOUNDARY STRENGTHS

Not all boundaries are equally strong — some are solid, some leaky, some nonexistent. Mapping them helps you see where your energy is protected and where it's vulnerable. This isn't judgment; it's insight.

Why it helps:
This exercise makes abstract boundaries tangible. It highlights where your nervous system feels unsafe and gives you concrete strategies to reinforce your limits. Seeing your boundary map builds confidence and helps you act intentionally rather than reactively.

List areas where you interact with your co-parent (e.g., drop-offs, texts, school events).
Rate each boundary's current strength on a scale of 1–10 (1 = completely porous, 10 = unshakable).
In the notes column, write what challenges or triggers make this boundary weaker (e.g., guilt, fear of conflict, manipulation).
Identify one small step to strengthen each weaker boundary (e.g., using text instead of calls, delaying a response, pre-writing what you want to say).

TRACING THE TRUTH

MAPPING YOUR BOUNDARY STRENGTHS

Boundary	Strength Level (1–10)	Notes/Triggers

CHECKPOINT

Relapsing On Your Boundaries

Boundary setting is a skill, not a one-time fix. If you find yourself slipping—responding emotionally, over-explaining, or retracting your boundaries—pause without judgment. Reflect on what triggered you and remind yourself that growth includes missteps. Revisit your scripts and grounding tools. Reach out to your support system. Remember: Every attempt strengthens your ability to protect your space.

TINY WINS PROTOCOL

When you're overwhelmed, your brain can trick you into believing nothing is possible. Big goals feel impossible, so you stall. But tiny actions build proof: I can move. Completing a single small task sparks dopamine — the brain's reward chemical — and that fuels momentum. Instead of waiting for motivation, you create it by acting first. Two-minute wins keep you out of the freeze state and remind you that forward movement doesn't need to be dramatic to matter. Over time, stacking these little completions can shift your entire day — and even your sense of self. It's not about doing everything; it's about proving to yourself that you can do something.

Pick a micro-task: Something that takes under 2 minutes (wash mug, text back, stretch, shower).

02 Countdown launch: Mental health awareness helps reduce stigma, promotes empathy, and encourages open conversations about mental health concerns.

03 Complete & log: Write it down or check it off for a small hit of satisfaction.

04 Notice momentum: Let the success energy carry you into the next doable action.

05 Repeat daily: Build trust with yourself through small, steady proof points.

THREE PILLARS BEFORE NOON

When you're caught in anxiety, depression, or burnout, your nervous system can swing between shutdown and overdrive. The quickest way to steady yourself is to touch three key areas: body, mind, and pleasure. Moving your body brings energy online; completing a mastery task (even something small like an email) restores a sense of competence; and engaging in pleasure reminds you that joy and safety are still accessible. This "trio" isn't about being productive — it's about balance. Think of it as a daily reset button. By noon, if you've already touched your body, completed one mastery task, and tasted one moment of pleasure, you've laid down anchors for resilience. Instead of asking your day to be perfect, you give yourself three touchpoints that prove: I can show up, I can accomplish, and I can enjoy.

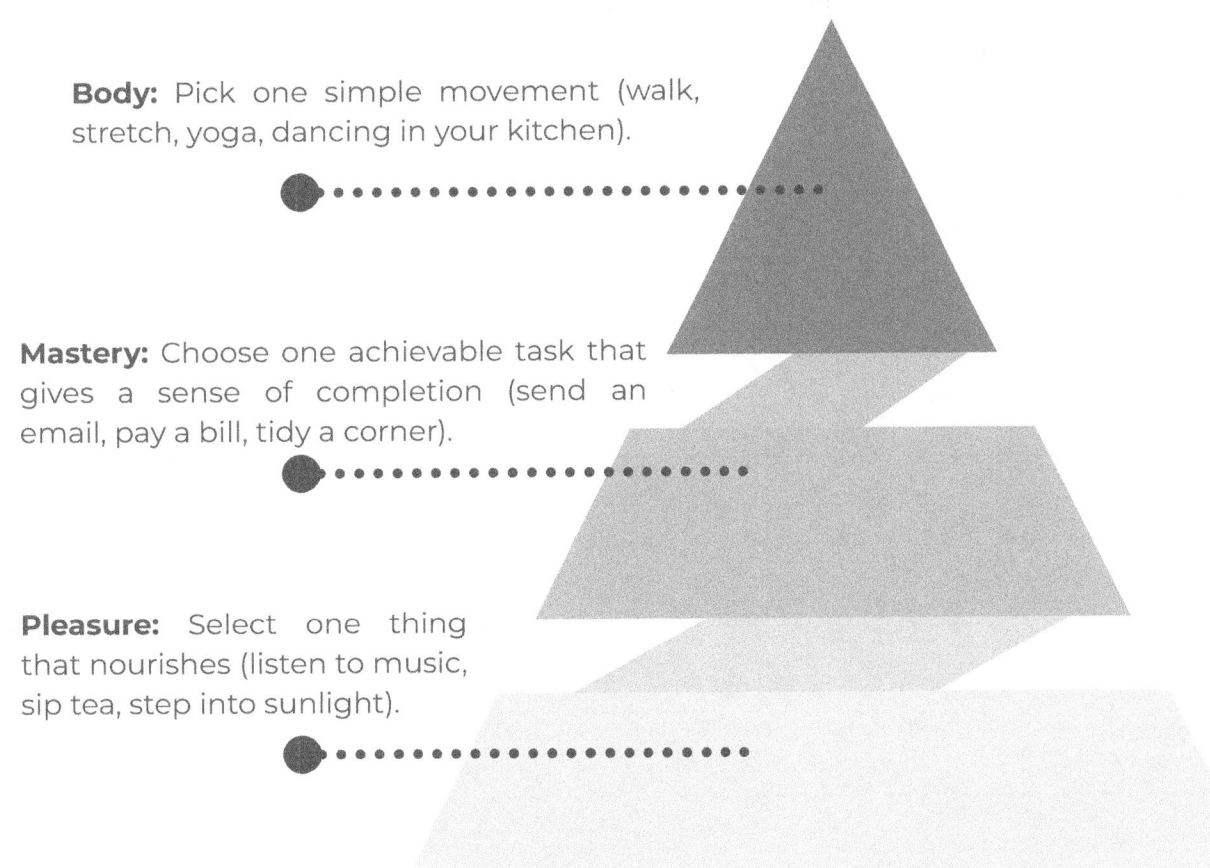

Body: Pick one simple movement (walk, stretch, yoga, dancing in your kitchen).

Mastery: Choose one achievable task that gives a sense of completion (send an email, pay a bill, tidy a corner).

Pleasure: Select one thing that nourishes (listen to music, sip tea, step into sunlight).

Stack them early: Aim to complete all three before noon to set your rhythm.

Reflect briefly: Notice how touching all three domains shifts your mood and energy.

Letters To Your Future Self

Write a letter from your future self who has mastered compassionate, firm boundaries with your co-parent. How does that future you describe your growth and peace? What advice do they give about staying strong?

Letters To Your Future Self

Letters To Your Future Self

BRINGING IT ALL TOGETHER

Notice how the skills you're learning connect and build on each other. This is where your learning starts to feel real and whole.

HOW DOES AN EARLIER SKILL OR INSIGHT RELATE TO WHAT YOU'RE LEARNING NOW?

CAN YOU SPOT MOMENTS WHERE THESE TOOLS OVERLAP OR SUPPORT EACH OTHER?

HOW MIGHT COMBINING THEM CREATE STRONGER RESULTS?

SECTION FOUR

The Guilt, Shame, and Self-Doubt of Parenting Through Abuse

Co-parenting with an emotional abuser often means carrying a heavy, invisible backpack filled with guilt, shame, and endless self-doubt. You might wonder if you're doing enough, if you're protecting your child well enough, or if your feelings are "justified" or "too much." These emotions swirl like a storm, sometimes overwhelming your sense of self and making every parenting decision feel like a test.

In this section, we'll gently unravel these feelings. You'll learn how guilt and shame have been woven into your co-parenting experience — often by the abuser's manipulation, but also by societal pressures and your own high standards as a parent. You'll be reminded that your worth isn't measured by their words or your toughest days, but by your love and commitment. Together, we'll build self-compassion and trust to counterbalance those relentless inner critics.

Making Sense Of It
Guilt, Shame, and the Emotional Architecture of Co-Parenting with an Abuser

Guilt and shame are heavy, but they're not evidence that you're failing. They're signals — your mind and body trying to help you survive a situation that isn't survivable without careful attention. Guilt often shows up first, whispering that you could have done more, been firmer, or kept the peace. Shame is louder, harsher, and trickier: it tells you that something about you is broken, that you are fundamentally flawed. When you're co-parenting with someone who manipulates, criticizes, or undermines, these feelings are constantly fueled from the outside. Subtle digs, last-minute disruptions, or emotional manipulation all tell your nervous system: danger. Over time, your body believes it, and your mind starts treating the abuser's judgments as your own.

Humans are wired to seek social validation — we evolved in tight-knit communities where approval meant safety and survival. Anthropologically, when our "tribe" responds with criticism, withdrawal, or indifference, we internalize it. Our brains don't differentiate between minor social stressors and life-threatening threats when these patterns repeat. This is why guilt and shame can feel overwhelming and persistent: they are your nervous system reacting to ongoing threat and relational tension.

Your guilt isn't proof that you're weak; it's proof that you care deeply about your child and want to protect them. Your shame isn't proof that you're broken; it's proof that your nervous system has been overexposed to judgment and manipulation. Both emotions are normal human responses to an abnormal, high-stakes situation.

Making Sense Of It
Guilt, Shame, and the Emotional Architecture of Co-Parenting with an Abuser

The real work is learning to see them for what they are: guides, not truths. Guilt highlights where your values and care are strongest. Shame flags where outside voices — the abuser's story — have tried to write over your own.

In practical terms, guilt and shame often operate as a loop in your nervous system. You replay interactions, overthink decisions, and second-guess yourself endlessly. These loops are not evidence of failure; they are your brain trying to prevent future harm in an environment where control was limited. Understanding this neurobiological pattern helps you step back with curiosity rather than judgment. It allows you to notice the "alarm bells" for what they are — not indictments of your character, but signals that your nervous system is processing complex, high-stakes relational stress.

Anthropologically, this makes sense: human beings survived because we learned from patterns of social reward and punishment. The problem is that in the modern context of ongoing abuse, these ancient survival circuits are hijacked. You're wired to respond as if you can still prevent the harm, even when the circumstances are largely out of your control. Recognizing this truth allows you to redirect energy from self-punishment to self-compassion. You can begin to nurture internal witnesses, build clear boundaries, and gently reassure yourself that being human — with all the complexity, contradictions, and mistakes that entails — is enough.

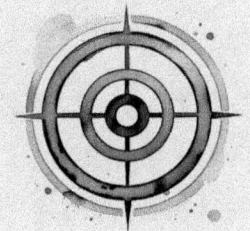# Trigger Check-In

> You sit alone after a difficult visit with your child and co-parent. The abuser's parting words echo in your mind: "You're making this harder than it needs to be." You question every decision you made during the visit — Were you too strict? Too soft? You feel a familiar ache of shame mixed with guilt, as if somehow you failed your child or yourself.

> I see the weight you carry — the constant questioning, the ache of not feeling good enough. I see the loneliness and the effort it takes to keep showing up for your child despite all this. Your love is fierce and real, and it's more than enough, even on your hardest days.

What are the most common messages of guilt or shame I hear from my co-parent or myself?

Identify specific phrases or beliefs that haunt you.

What are the most common messages of guilt or shame I hear from my co-parent or myself?

How do guilt and shame show up physically in my body during or after co-parenting interactions?

Describe sensations, tension, or fatigue.

How do guilt and shame show up physically in my body during or after co-parenting interactions?

In what ways have I internalized blame for the co-parenting challenges I face?

Reflect on what parts of the problem you carry.

In what ways have I internalized blame for the co-parenting challenges I face?

How does guilt motivate me, and how does it limit me?

Explore the double-edged nature of guilt in your life.

How does guilt motivate me, and how does it limit me?

What would it feel like to release shame and replace it with self-compassion?

Imagine a kinder inner voice guiding you.

What would it feel like to release shame and replace it with self-compassion?

How can I recognize when I'm taking responsibility for things outside my control?

Identify boundaries between your role and your co-parent's behavior.

How can I recognize when I'm taking responsibility for things outside my control?

What small acts of forgiveness can I offer myself related to parenting struggles?

List ways to soften self-judgment.

What small acts of forgiveness can I offer myself related to parenting struggles?

How can I celebrate my strengths as a parent, even in difficult circumstances?

Recall moments when you've acted with courage, patience, or love.

How can I celebrate my strengths as a parent, even in difficult circumstances?

TRACING THE TRUTH

LETTERS TO SHAME AND SELF-COMPASSION

Shame thrives in silence and secrecy. Writing directly to it — and responding with compassion — gives your nervous system a chance to witness and release it.

Why it helps:
This exercise breaks the silent power of shame, creating space for self-compassion. It allows your nervous system to hear validation, shifts internalized narratives, and strengthens the inner witness — the part of you that remembers your efforts and your value despite abuse.

On one page, write a short letter from Shame to You. Let it say everything it usually whispers or shouts: "You're failing," "You can't do this," "You're a bad parent." Don't censor.
On the next page, write a response from your compassionate self, the part that sees your effort, values, and humanity. Include reminders like: "I see how hard you're trying," "Your love matters more than your mistakes," "You are not your abuser's story."
Read both letters aloud or to yourself. Notice your body's response.

TRACING THE TRUTH

LETTERS TO SHAME AND SELF-COMPASSION

TRACING THE TRUTH

LETTERS TO SHAME AND SELF-COMPASSION

TRACING THE TRUTH

LETTERS TO SHAME AND SELF-COMPASSION

TRACING THE TRUTH

THE GUILT VS. TRUTH TABLE

Guilt can feel overwhelming because it's often tangled with assumptions, "shoulds," and external expectations. This exercise helps you separate the stories your mind is telling from the grounded truth of your actions and intentions.

Why it helps:
This exercise externalizes guilt, revealing when it's a narrative your mind is spinning rather than a reflection of reality. It strengthens self-awareness, builds perspective, and reminds you that care, effort, and presence matter more than perfection.

In the Guilt Stories column, write every thought or feeling of guilt you're carrying about co-parenting. Examples: "I should have done more," "I shouldn't have yelled," "I failed my child."
In the Evidence & Truth column, counter each story with facts or observations. Example: "I made sure dinner was on time," "I set a boundary even when it was uncomfortable," "I kept my child safe and loved."
Reflect on the difference between what you feel and what actually happened. Circle any guilt that isn't supported by facts.

TRACING THE TRUTH

THE GUILT VS. TRUTH TABLE

Guilt Stories	**Evidence & Truth**

TRACING THE TRUTH

THE GUILT VS. TRUTH TABLE

Guilt Stories   **Evidence & Truth**

CHECKPOINT

Slipping Into Guilt Again

It's common to slip into guilt and shame, especially after a hard co-parenting day or a triggering comment. When this happens, remind yourself: feelings don't equal facts. Use your reframing tools and self-talk. Reach out to a trusted friend or therapist if possible. Healing is non-linear, and every compassionate choice strengthens your resilience.

MOOD MAPPING BY THE HOUR

Our mood is never random — it's deeply influenced by what we do, when we do it, and how our nervous system responds. When depression or anxiety is heavy, it can feel like nothing makes a difference. This log helps you prove to yourself that even small activities shift your emotional state, sometimes by just one point. And that one-point lift matters — it's momentum, a reminder that you aren't stuck forever. By tracking your mood alongside your activities, you build a personalized map of what nourishes you. Instead of relying on guesswork, you'll have hard evidence of your own resilience patterns. Over time, this practice shows you that certain choices (a call with a safe friend, a walk outside, finishing a task) consistently bring relief. This isn't about forcing happiness — it's about noticing what gently nudges you toward better.

For one day, each hour, write down what you're doing and your mood (0–10).

Repeat for a few days — notice patterns.

Circle activities that reliably lift you by at least one point.

Intentionally schedule more of those "one-point lifts" into your week.

Revisit the log whenever you feel stuck, to remind yourself you have options.

Day	Activity	Mood Before	Mood After

MOOD MAPPING BY THE HOUR

Day	Activity	Mood Before	Mood After

Letters To My Future Self

Write a letter from your future self who has learned to replace guilt and shame with kindness and strength. What wisdom do they share about parenting through abuse?

Letters To Your Future Self

SECTION FIVE

Managing Emotional Hijacks: Regulating Yourself When Triggered

Co-parenting with an emotional abuser often means walking through a minefield of triggers — sudden comments, tone shifts, or unexpected demands that send your nervous system into overdrive. These moments can feel like emotional hijacks: your body and mind snap into fight, flight, or freeze before you even realize what's happening. You might yell, shut down, or replay the event for hours, feeling powerless to stop the spiral.

This section is about reclaiming your nervous system — learning to recognize your triggers and respond with tools that help you regulate in real time. You'll discover practical, trauma-sensitive strategies including breathwork, DBT distress tolerance, and grounding exercises designed specifically for the unique stresses of co-parenting abuse. These tools will help you pause, calm the storm inside, and respond with clarity and strength, even when your co-parent pushes your buttons.

You don't have to be at the mercy of your triggers. With practice, you can regain control of your body, mind, and emotions — turning moments of chaos into opportunities for healing.

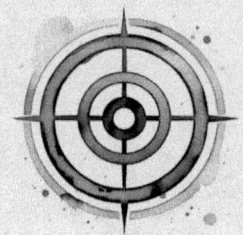 Trigger Check-In

You're on a call arranging next week's visit. Your co-parent suddenly accuses you of being "uncooperative" and "making things harder than they have to be." Your chest tightens, your breath quickens, and your mind floods with defensive thoughts. You feel the urge to argue or hang up, but instead, you pause, place your hand on your heart, and focus on slow, deep breaths. You remind yourself: this is a trigger, not the truth. You choose to respond calmly.

I see how terrifying it feels when your body betrays you with overwhelming emotions. I see the courage it takes to pause and choose differently. Your reactions are not failures — they are survival responses trying to keep you safe. You are learning new ways to respond, and that is powerful.

Making Sense Of It
When Triggers Hijack the Nervous System

Co-parenting with an emotional abuser is not just a logistical challenge—it's a constant negotiation between your body and your brain. Your nervous system, honed over millennia to detect subtle threats in social hierarchies, is on high alert. Every abrupt text, last-minute plan change, or veiled criticism can register as a signal of danger, even if rationally you know you're not in immediate harm. Anthropologically, humans evolved to survive in small, interdependent communities where social missteps could carry real consequences; today, your body interprets relational instability through the same ancient lens.

These responses are not failures of character—they are biological adaptations. Cortisol spikes, heart rate accelerates, muscles tighten, and your attention narrows, prioritizing survival over reflection. In trauma bonds, the loop becomes chronic: the body remains primed for threat even in calm moments, and every interaction is filtered through this lens of hypervigilance. Over time, this creates what psychologists call a "state of anticipatory stress," where you live partially in the past (replaying incidents) and partially in the future (preparing for the next conflict), leaving little room to simply exist in the present.

The complexity is compounded when the abuser alternates between aggression and occasional warmth. Your nervous system becomes trained to predict reward from threat—a hallmark of intermittent reinforcement.

Making Sense Of It
When Triggers Hijack the Nervous System

Neuroscience shows that these patterns create deeply ingrained neural pathways, making it harder to disentangle your reactions from the stimulus. You might catch yourself snapping at your child, freezing during a conversation, or obsessively replaying a text—these are not signs that you're failing as a parent; they are evidence of a nervous system doing exactly what it evolved to do: protect.

Healing begins with awareness and curiosity. Naming the physical sensations in your body—tight chest, shallow breath, clenched jaw—is the first step in breaking the autopilot response. Unlike previous advice about boundaries or reflective exercises, here we focus on mapping patterns: observing when triggers appear, noting how your body responds, and recognizing recurring cycles. This mapping doesn't blame you—it externalizes the biology, separates the signal from the judgment, and allows you to practice choice.

Over time, deliberate interventions—breathwork, brief grounding, and mental rehearsal—teach the nervous system that not every trigger requires full mobilization. This is not suppression or denial; it's retraining your body to distinguish between immediate threat and emotional provocation. Anthropologically, this mirrors how early humans would signal "all clear" to their community, re-establishing safety after a threat. In your modern context, micro-moments of self-regulation send the same message to your nervous system: you are safe, your child is safe, and you can respond rather than react.

Making Sense Of It
When Triggers Hijack the Nervous System

The goal is integration. By observing patterns, naming physical cues, and practicing intentional responses, you begin to reclaim agency over the moments that used to hijack you. This work isn't linear—it's a practice of patience, compassion, and steady attention. Your nervous system may resist at first, but each pause, each breath, each conscious choice rewires the brain, strengthening pathways that favor presence, clarity, and resilience. In a situation where control is limited, this is one of the most powerful ways to reclaim your power—not through confrontation, but through self-awareness and embodied trust.

What are my most common emotional triggers related to co-parenting?

Identify specific words, tones, or situations that activate your nervous system.

What are my most common emotional triggers related to co-parenting?

How does my body feel when I'm triggered?

Describe physical sensations—tightness, racing heart, nausea, etc.

How does my body feel when I'm triggered?

What patterns do I notice in my reactions (fight, flight, freeze)?

Reflect on how you tend to respond under stress.

What patterns do I notice in my reactions (fight, flight, freeze)?

When have I successfully used a calming strategy during or after a trigger?

Recall what worked and how it felt.

When have I successfully used a calming strategy during or after a trigger?

How might I prepare for challenging interactions to reduce emotional hijacks?

Plan self-care or mental rehearsals before contact.

How might I prepare for challenging interactions to reduce emotional hijacks?

What does it feel like when I allow myself to pause instead of reacting immediately?

Describe any shifts in perspective or emotion.

What does it feel like when I allow myself to pause instead of reacting immediately?

How can I integrate breathwork or grounding into my daily routine?

Brainstorm simple practices to build resilience.

How can I integrate breathwork or grounding into my daily routine?

What compassionate messages can I say to myself when I struggle to regulate?

Create affirmations or reminders that soothe.

What compassionate messages can I say to myself when I struggle to regulate?

TRACING THE TRUTH

TRIGGER MAPPING TABLE

Understanding your triggers is the first step toward reclaiming control. This exercise helps you see patterns without judgment and notice how your body reacts in real time.

Why it helps:
Seeing patterns externalized on paper turns invisible stress into tangible information. It creates space between stimulus and reaction, helping your nervous system learn it's safe to pause rather than immediately react.

Examine the three columns:
Trigger/Interaction → e.g., text from co-parent, last-minute cancellation
Body Response → e.g., tight chest, racing heart, shallow breath
Possible Response/Choice → e.g., pause and breathe, step away, journal thoughts

Over a week, fill in the table whenever you notice a strong emotional reaction. Be honest and specific.
After a week, review the table: notice which triggers recur, how your body responds, and where intentional choices helped reduce escalation.

TRACING THE TRUTH

TRIGGER MAPPING TABLE

Trigger/Interaction	Body Response	Possible Response/Choice

TRACING THE TRUTH

TRIGGER MAPPING TABLE

Trigger/Interaction **Body Response** **Possible Response/Choice**

CHECKPOINT

Emotional Highjacks

It's okay if emotional hijacks sometimes win. If you react in ways you regret, practice radical acceptance—acknowledge the slip without judgment. Use your grounding and breathwork tools to recover quickly. Reflect on what led to the hijack and what early signs you missed. Every moment of self-awareness deepens your healing.

SELF-COMPASSION BREAK

When stress, shame, or pain flare up, most of us go straight into self-criticism: Why can't I handle this better? What's wrong with me? That inner attack only tightens the spiral. Kristin Neff's Self-Compassion Break interrupts that cycle. It gives you three small handholds: recognition of your pain, the reminder you're not alone in it, and an active choice to soften instead of harden against yourself. With repetition, your nervous system learns that you don't have to white-knuckle through suffering or numb out — you can meet yourself with the same tenderness you'd extend to a friend. That shift doesn't erase the pain, but it changes the way it lands in your body. Over time, it builds resilience, because you're no longer abandoned in hard moments; you become your own safe ally.

Notice —
Pause and acknowledge: "This is hard. This hurts."

Kindness —
Place a hand on your chest or cheek and whisper: "May I be gentle with myself right now."

Common Humanity —
Say: "Others feel this too. I'm not the only one struggling."

POCKET MOOD LIFTERS

When life feels heavy, it's easy to forget what actually helps. In hard moments, the brain tends to focus on what's wrong, not what's available. An Antidote List is your preloaded reminder: ten small, proven things that shift your state even a little. These aren't grand fixes or instant cures — they're micro-adjustments that keep you from sliding deeper into the stuckness. Pairing an antidote before a hard task helps you face it with steadier energy; using one after provides recovery and closure so you don't carry the weight forward. Over time, this list becomes muscle memory — your nervous system learns, When I struggle, I have options. That's the opposite of hopelessness.

1 **List Ten —** Write down 10 things that reliably lift your mood (a song, a walk, fresh air, texting a safe friend, lighting a candle). Keep them small and doable.

....

....

....

....

....

....

....

2 **Use Before —** Pick one before facing a task you tend to dread. Let it soften resistance.

3 **Use After —** Choose another as a closing ritual. Let it tell your body, That part is done. I'm safe again.

Letters To Your Future Self

Write a letter from your future self who handles triggers with calm and clarity. What encouragement do they give you about managing emotional hijacks in co-parenting?

Letters To Your Future Self

SECTION SIX

Navigating Conflict Without Losing Yourself

Co-parenting with an emotional abuser means conflict isn't a rare event—it's a frequent, exhausting reality. These conflicts aren't just disagreements; they can quickly spiral into manipulations, blame, or emotional warfare that leave you feeling drained, doubting yourself, or even frozen. The stakes feel high because your child's wellbeing depends on how you both manage these moments.

This section offers you a trauma-informed roadmap for navigating conflict with your co-parent without losing your sense of self or your emotional balance. You'll learn how to recognize escalating patterns, de-escalate tense situations, and engage in communication that prioritizes safety and respect—both for you and your child. You'll also receive practical "How to Respond" scripts to maintain your boundaries and protect your nervous system in real time. Conflict doesn't have to define your co-parenting journey. With these strategies, you'll develop tools to keep your center, even when chaos surrounds you.

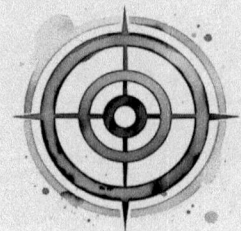

Trigger Check-In

During a pickup, your co-parent accuses you of "making everything difficult" in front of your child. Your chest tightens, and your first instinct is to defend yourself. Instead, you take a slow breath, keep your voice steady, and say, "I'm focused on what's best for our child. Let's keep the conversation respectful." You then remove yourself calmly from the situation, giving space to cool down.

I see how hard it is to face conflict when you've been hurt so deeply. I see the courage it takes to hold your ground and protect your child's emotional safety. You're learning how to be firm without being harsh, steady without shutting down. That balance is a radical act of care for yourself and your child.

Making Sense Of It
The Neurobiology of Conflict and Calm

Conflict isn't just a mental or verbal experience—it's a full-body event. When you interact with an emotional abuser, your nervous system interprets their words, tone, or behavior as a potential threat. Your brain's ancient survival circuitry—rooted in the amygdala and limbic system—activates before your conscious mind has a chance to reason. Heart rate spikes, muscles tighten, breath shortens, and attention narrows. This fight, flight, or freeze response is not a flaw; it's your biology doing exactly what it evolved to do: protect you.

Past trauma compounds this effect. Your nervous system carries memory of prior danger, betrayal, or emotional unpredictability, so even small provocations can feel catastrophic. Your logical brain, housed in the prefrontal cortex, struggles to regain control because it's literally competing with a body that believes it's under attack. Understanding this helps you see that reactive outbursts, shutdowns, or anxiety aren't failures—they're survival signals.

Conflict with a co-parent is uniquely complicated because the stakes involve your child, shared responsibilities, and unavoidable contact. This ongoing exposure keeps your nervous system in a low-level state of alert, even when nothing immediately threatening occurs. Your body is essentially scanning for danger constantly, which is exhausting—but knowing this gives you power. Awareness is the first step toward reclaiming choice, rather than reacting unconsciously to every trigger.

Making Sense Of It
The Neurobiology of Conflict and Calm

De-escalation is a way to retrain this system. When you notice your chest tightening, breath shortening, or thoughts spinning, you can intervene before the response spirals. Techniques like grounding through the senses, neutral phrasing, pausing before responding, or physically stepping away signal to your nervous system: "I am safe. I am present. Danger is not immediate." These small interventions are neurobiological micro-repairs—they calm your amygdala, activate your parasympathetic nervous system, and give your prefrontal cortex room to make intentional choices.

Over time, repeated, consistent practice creates a new neural pattern. Your body begins to recognize that conflict does not always equal danger. Calm responses, clear boundaries, and measured communication gradually become your default, rather than a constant state of hypervigilance. You are reclaiming control—not by controlling your co-parent, but by regulating your own nervous system. In doing so, you protect your emotional space, model safety for your child, and honor your own biology in the process.

Finally, it's important to remember that de-escalation isn't about perfection—it's about presence. Each moment you respond from a grounded, intentional space is a small act of repair, not just for your nervous system, but for your child's experience of safety and trust. Your capacity to stay calm, even under provocation, sends a powerful, nonverbal message: stability exists, even in chaos. That is not just survival—it is a quiet, profound reclaiming of your power, your peace, and your humanity.

What physical signs do I notice when conflict with my co-parent starts to escalate?

Track your body's early warning signals.

What physical signs do I notice when conflict with my co-parent starts to escalate?

How do I typically respond to conflict—fight, flight, or freeze?

Reflect honestly on your patterns.

How do I typically respond to conflict—fight, flight, or freeze?

What language or behaviors from my co-parent trigger me the most?

Identify specific triggers to anticipate.

What language or behaviors from my co-parent trigger me the most?

How can I use calm, neutral language to de-escalate tense moments?

Brainstorm phrases or approaches.

How can I use calm, neutral language to de-escalate tense moments?

What boundaries can I set during conflict to protect my emotional space?

List limits around tone, timing, or topics.

What boundaries can I set during conflict to protect my emotional space?

When might stepping away from a conflict be the healthiest choice?

Visualize how to do this with grace and safety.

When might stepping away from a conflict be the healthiest choice?

How can I model respectful conflict resolution for my child?

Reflect on the example you want to set.

How can I model respectful conflict resolution for my child?

What support or self-care do I need after a conflict interaction?

Plan concrete ways to restore balance.

What support or self-care do I need after a conflict interaction?

TRACING THE TRUTH

CONFLICT RESPONSE TABLE FOR DE-ESCALATION

Tracking interactions helps you see where conflict tends to spiral and where intentional responses successfully calm the situation.

Why it helps:
Reflection reinforces what works, builds awareness of triggers, and trains your nervous system to remain regulated during stressful interactions.

Examine the table on the next page.
Trigger/Conflict Event – Describe what happened, who said or did what, and the context.
Automatic Reaction – Note your emotional and physical response (fight, flight, freeze).
De-escalation Response – Write what you did or could have done to calm the situation: neutral phrasing, time-out, breathing, or redirecting the conversation.

After each interaction, fill in the table honestly—this is a reflection, not judgment.
Review the table weekly to notice patterns: which triggers consistently escalate, and which responses successfully de-escalate.
Adjust your strategies over time, and celebrate even small victories in staying regulated.

TRACING THE TRUTH

CONFLICT RESPONSE TABLE FOR DE-ESCALATION

Trigger/Conflict **Automatic Reaction** **De-escalation Response**

TRACING THE TRUTH

CONFLICT RESPONSE TABLE FOR DE-ESCALATION

Trigger/Conflict　　　**Automatic Reaction**　　　**De-escalation Response**

TRACING THE TRUTH

CONFLICT RESPONSE TABLE FOR DE-ESCALATION

Trigger/Conflict **Automatic Reaction** **De-escalation Response**

TRACING THE TRUTH

THE DE-ESCALATION TRIGGER CIRCLE

Before conflict escalates, your nervous system gives subtle signals. Mapping these early signs helps you intervene and maintain calm.

Why it helps:
Recognizing your body's warning signs allows you to act before the fight, flight, or freeze response takes over. By pairing triggers with intentional de-escalation strategies, you train your nervous system to respond rather than react.

Examine the circle in the middle of the next page titled "De-escalation Triggers."
From the circle, draw 6–8 lines outward. At the end of each line, write a specific trigger: e.g., a certain tone, sudden demand, criticism, or last-minute change in plans.
Along each line, note your physical reactions: racing heart, shallow breath, clenched jaw, tight stomach.
Next to each physical cue, write a de-escalation action you can take: pause, deep breath, neutral language, brief time-out, grounding through senses.
Keep the circle visible. Review and refine it as you discover new triggers or effective strategies.

TRACING THE TRUTH

THE DE-ESCALATION TRIGGER CIRCLE

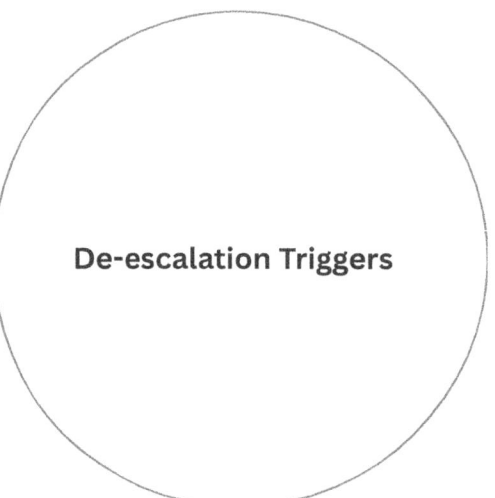

CHECKPOINT

Getting Into Trigger Cycles

If you find yourself caught in a reactive cycle—raising your voice, shutting down, or feeling overwhelmed—remember this is part of healing. Acknowledge the moment without judgment, use grounding techniques, and practice self-compassion. Reflect later on what triggered the escalation and how you might respond differently next time. Each step toward calm is progress.

MY SAFETY NET

In moments of overwhelm, your nervous system isn't wired to pause and think through options — it leaps into fight, flight, or freeze. A written safety plan is like a ready-made anchor: instead of spiraling or going blank, you have a clear map back to calm. By identifying your unique triggers, early warning signs, and support network ahead of time, you create a sense of control and reassurance. This is less about predicting every crisis and more about telling your body and mind: I have a way back.

Identify triggers: Write down situations, phrases, or tones of voice that tend to spark distress.

Notice early warning signs: List how your body tells you stress is rising (racing heart, clenched jaw, shallow breath).

Choose three rapid-calm skills: Breathing, grounding, or movement tools you can use quickly.

Name two safe people: Write their contact info. Keep the plan somewhere visible or carry a copy with you.

SAFE PEOPLE

CALM SKILLS

TRIGGERS & WARNING SIGNS

WINDOW OF TOLERANCE MAP

When you're dysregulated — whether spun up with racing thoughts or shut down and numb — it's almost impossible to think clearly. Mapping your "window of tolerance" gives you a visual reminder of what your nervous system looks and feels like when it's balanced, overstimulated, or under-engaged. Instead of feeling hijacked, you can recognize: "Ah, I'm outside my window right now." That awareness alone widens your choices. It also keeps you from turning regulation into a guessing game; you'll have a personal roadmap of cues and tools that work for you.

Fill in personal cues. For each state, jot what you notice in your body, thoughts, and emotions. (Example: Hyper = clenched jaw, racing mind. Hypo = heavy limbs, flat affect.)

Add regulation tools. Next to Hyper, write 2–3 down-regulating skills (ex: slow breathing, grounding). Next to Hypo, add up-regulating ones (ex: movement, music).

Calm/Present (your window)	Hyper (revved-up)	Hypo (shut-down)
	↑	↓

Regulation Tools

Letters To My Future Self

Write a letter from your future self who manages conflict with calm and clarity. What encouragement and wisdom do they offer about staying grounded in difficult conversations?

Letters To Your Future Self

BRINGING IT ALL TOGETHER

Notice how the skills you're learning connect and build on each other. This is where your learning starts to feel real and whole.

HOW DOES AN EARLIER SKILL OR INSIGHT RELATE TO WHAT YOU'RE LEARNING NOW?

CAN YOU SPOT MOMENTS WHERE THESE TOOLS OVERLAP OR SUPPORT EACH OTHER?

HOW MIGHT COMBINING THEM CREATE STRONGER RESULTS?

SECTION SEVEN

When Co-Parenting Triggers Old Wounds — Healing Your Inner Child

Co-parenting with an emotional abuser often feels like walking through a hall of mirrors — every interaction reflecting back not only present challenges but echoes of past pain. Old wounds from childhood, past relationships, or your own upbringing can resurface with a fierce intensity, triggered by your co-parent's behaviors or words. These moments can leave you feeling vulnerable, overwhelmed, or stuck in patterns that feel impossible to break.

In this section, we lean gently into those old wounds with kindness and curiosity, learning how co-parenting can stir your inner child — the part of you that still needs safety, love, and validation. Recognizing when you're triggered at this deeper level is key to interrupting cycles of shame, guilt, or self-blame. You'll discover practical tools to soothe and nurture your inner child while staying grounded in your adult self. This is where real healing begins — in the tender space between past pain and present strength.

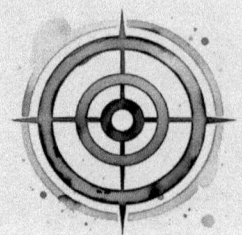

Trigger Check-In

You receive a sharp, dismissive text from your co-parent, and suddenly, you're not just upset — you feel small, unseen, like the little kid who once felt ignored or criticized. You want to lash out or shut down, but instead, you pause and ask yourself, "What does my inner child need right now?" You picture holding that scared child with kindness, offering comfort instead of judgment.

I see the tender parts of you that ache beneath the surface, the parts you've had to protect or hide. I see how those wounds make co-parenting harder, stirring up fears and pain that aren't about today but still live inside you. You are worthy of care and safety — especially from yourself.

Making Sense Of It
When Past Wounds Surface in the Present

Your nervous system doesn't respond only to the stress happening right now—it also carries echoes of old hurts, disappointments, and unresolved fear. With an emotionally challenging co-parent, these old wounds can surface in surprising ways. A curt email, a canceled plan, or a subtle critique might trigger more than frustration—they can awaken memories of past neglect, rejection, or the times you felt unseen, unsafe, or "not enough." Suddenly, a situation that seems manageable on the surface can feel overwhelming, tangled, and impossible to navigate. The intensity of your emotional reactions often isn't about what's happening in the moment—it's about layers of experience your nervous system is trying to process all at once.

This is where the concept of the "inner child" becomes useful. It represents the parts of you that still carry the sensations, fears, and unmet needs of your past—not as a sign of weakness, but as an insight into your emotional wiring. When these parts are activated, you might notice sudden waves of anxiety, shame, guilt, or self-criticism that don't fully fit the present. These feelings are your nervous system signaling that old patterns of threat and protection are blending with current stress. Anthropologically, humans are wired to respond this way: our brains are designed to predict danger based on past experience. It's an adaptive survival mechanism that can feel overwhelming when the danger is psychological rather than physical.

Making Sense Of It
When Past Wounds Surface in the Present

Recognizing these patterns helps you shift from self-blame to self-awareness. You can witness the old fears without being controlled by them. Compassionate attention to your inner child—listening to its fears, naming its sadness, and offering reassurance—helps the nervous system recalibrate. It allows your adult self to respond intentionally rather than reactively, bringing clarity, boundaries, and calm to high-stress interactions.

Over time, these practices foster emotional resilience. The adult and inner child parts of yourself begin to coexist, creating a richer internal dialogue that allows you to navigate conflict without becoming consumed by it. You learn that feeling triggered doesn't make you broken—it makes you human. You learn to give yourself permission to experience complex emotions simultaneously, to honor both vulnerability and strength, and to respond to co-parenting challenges from a grounded, empowered place. This is how you learn to trust your instincts, and transform old patterns of fear.

By recognizing the universality of these reactions, you also normalize your experience. You are not alone in feeling the weight of past trauma intertwined with present responsibilities. Many caregivers, survivors, and parents carry similar layers of history while trying to protect and nurture those they love. This understanding opens a bridge from isolation to connection: it tells you that your nervous system's reactions are natural, your emotions are valid, and your capacity for compassion—for yourself and your child—is immense.

When do I notice my inner child getting triggered during co-parenting interactions?

Explore specific moments and feelings.

When do I notice my inner child getting triggered during co-parenting interactions?

What unmet needs from my childhood might be surfacing now?

Reflect on what safety, love, or validation you longed for then.

What unmet needs from my childhood might be surfacing now?

How do I currently respond to these inner child triggers?

Notice patterns of self-criticism, avoidance, or emotional flooding.

How do I currently respond to these inner child triggers?

What would it feel like to respond to my inner child with kindness and compassion?

Imagine comforting and nurturing that part of yourself.

What would it feel like to respond to my inner child with kindness and compassion?

How can I create safe space for my inner child during difficult co-parenting moments?

List soothing practices or self-care rituals.

How can I create safe space for my inner child during difficult co-parenting moments?

What messages did I receive growing up about parenting, conflict, or emotions?

Identify beliefs that might influence your current experience.

What messages did I receive growing up about parenting, conflict, or emotions?

How can I gently challenge or reframe those beliefs to support my healing?

Write alternative, supportive messages for yourself.

How can I gently challenge or reframe those beliefs to support my healing?

What small acts of kindness can I offer my inner child today?

Brainstorm daily rituals to nurture your emotional wellbeing.

What small acts of kindness can I offer my inner child today?

Letters To Your Future Self

Write a letter from your future self who holds your inner child with steady love and strength. What encouragement do they offer about honoring your past while moving forward?

Letters To Your Future Self

Letters To Your Future Self

POCKET OF SAFETY

When stress hits, your nervous system automatically searches for threat. Resource installation interrupts that loop by giving your body a felt reminder of safety, strength, or care. Instead of only rehearsing pain, you practice anchoring to something nurturing and stabilizing. This isn't about pretending the hard stuff doesn't exist — it's about teaching your brain and body that safety and support also exist. By pairing the memory with a body cue (like placing your hand on your heart), you create a portable anchor you can return to whenever you feel unsteady. Over time, this strengthens your capacity to self-soothe and widen your window of tolerance.

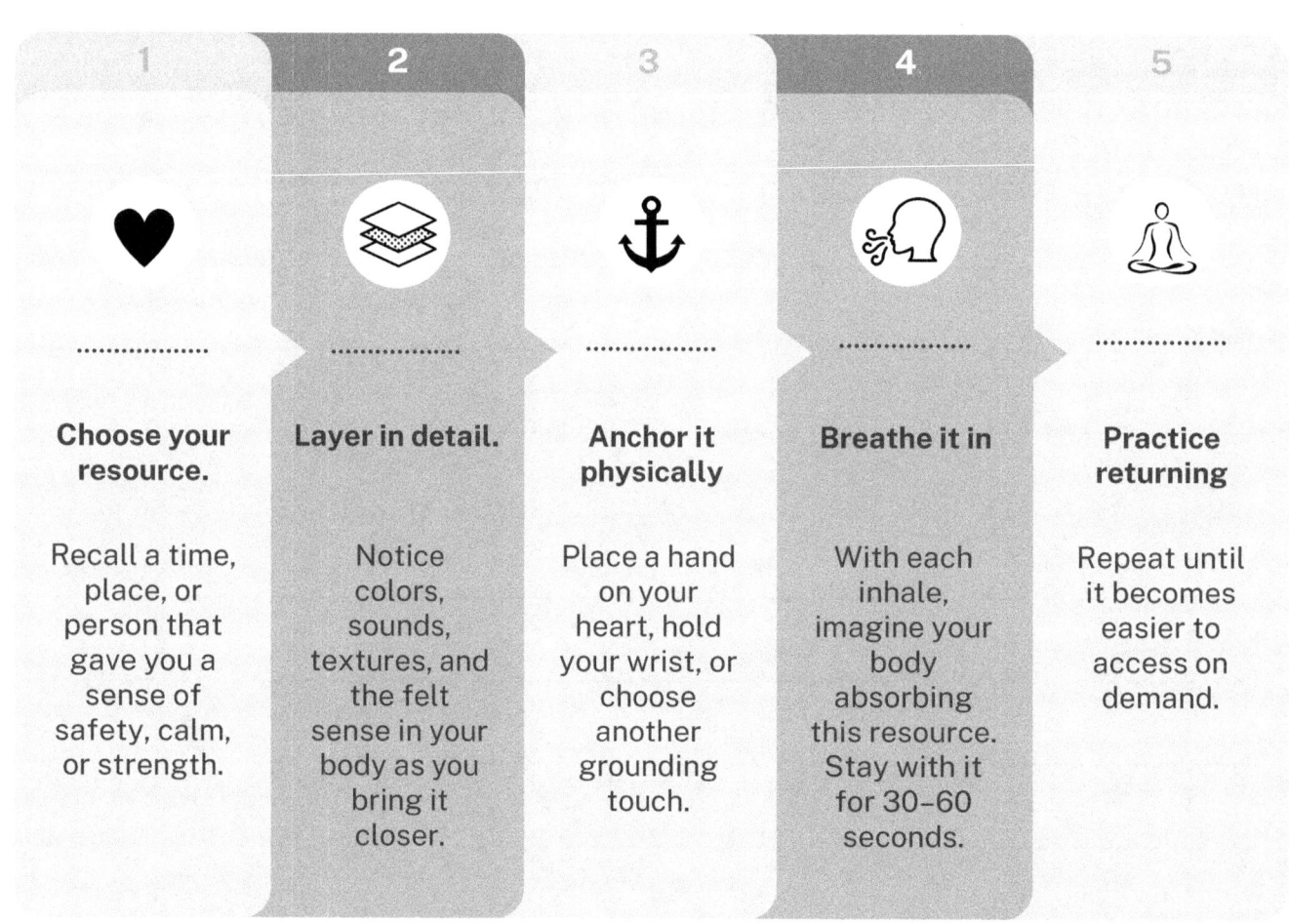

1. Choose your resource.
Recall a time, place, or person that gave you a sense of safety, calm, or strength.

2. Layer in detail.
Notice colors, sounds, textures, and the felt sense in your body as you bring it closer.

3. Anchor it physically
Place a hand on your heart, hold your wrist, or choose another grounding touch.

4. Breathe it in
With each inhale, imagine your body absorbing this resource. Stay with it for 30–60 seconds.

5. Practice returning
Repeat until it becomes easier to access on demand.

PREPPING FOR TRIGGERS

Triggers often feel like they ambush you out of nowhere. But the truth is, many of them are predictable. By anticipating where you might get pulled off-center, you remove the element of surprise — and that's half the battle. A trigger plan sets you up with choice: which skills you'll lean on, what words you'll use, and how you'll protect yourself if things get too intense. Instead of being at the mercy of the moment, you walk in knowing you have backup. The post-event debrief closes the loop, helping your nervous system learn that you can encounter stress and recover, without slipping into shame. This practice builds confidence, resilience, and the quiet reminder that you're not powerless — you're prepared.

01. Predict

Think about the upcoming event. What likely triggers might show up? Write them down.

Pick two calming or grounding strategies you know work for you (breathing, stepping outside, orienting).

02. Choose skills

03. Script yourself

Prepare one short phrase you can use if you need to step back (e.g., "I need a minute, I'll be right back.").

Decide where you can go if you need space — outside, bathroom, car, or even leaving entirely.

04. Exit plan

05. Debrief with kindness

Afterward, check in with yourself. What worked? What was hard? Offer compassion, not critique.

SECTION EIGHT

Healing the Trauma Bond — Breaking Free Within Co-Parenting

Co-parenting with an emotional abuser often means living inside a trauma bond — a powerful, confusing connection that keeps pulling you back, even when you know it's harmful. Trauma bonds are built on cycles of pain and relief, control and care, hope and heartbreak. They play tricks on your heart and mind, making it hard to step back or see clearly.

This section helps you recognize the trauma bond's subtle and overt ways of holding you captive, even when physical separation isn't possible. You'll gain tools to loosen its grip, heal from its pull, and reclaim your autonomy and peace — all while navigating co-parenting. These strategies aren't about cutting ties completely (that's often impossible), but about breaking the emotional chains that keep you stuck.

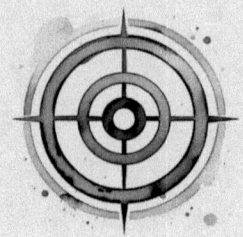 Trigger Check-In

After a particularly tense exchange, your co-parent unexpectedly sends a message that feels warm and caring. Your heart races, hope blooms, and for a moment, you forget the pain. But soon after, the cycle repeats, leaving you exhausted and confused. You recognize this pattern now and decide to journal about what you're feeling instead of rushing to respond.

I see how deeply conflicting it is to want safety and connection while also needing to protect yourself. I see the exhaustion of loving someone who hurts you, and the strength it takes to hold space for your child and your healing. You are not weak — you are navigating a complicated dance with courage.

Making Sense Of It
The Complicated Web of Trauma Bonds in Co-Parenting

Trauma bonds are not just about love or loyalty—they're about survival. They form when unpredictability, fear, and intermittent kindness create a cycle that your nervous system learns to crave. Moments of connection, warmth, or cooperation are magnified precisely because they are so rare, making the subsequent tension or conflict feel unbearable. This is the same mechanism that drives addiction: the brain's reward system becomes entangled with relief and hope, keeping you tethered to someone who also triggers fear, frustration, or pain.

In co-parenting with an emotionally abusive partner, trauma bonds are particularly complicated. You can't simply walk away. Unlike a romantic relationship that ends with distance, your child creates a living bridge that connects you to your co-parent, whether you like it or not. You carry the emotional labor of shielding your child, maintaining routines, and mediating conflict, all while navigating the unpredictable currents of an abusive partner's behavior. Meanwhile, your child may develop their own trauma bond with the other parent—a mix of attachment, fear, hope, and confusion—which adds another layer of tension. Their loyalty, love, and dependency become intertwined with your partner's volatile behavior, and you witness the push-pull dynamic without the ability to separate entirely.

This dual layer of attachment creates a bind: you want to protect your child and preserve your own wellbeing, yet your nervous system remains on alert, pulled into the highs and lows of your co-parent's inconsistent behavior.

Making Sense Of It The Complicated Web of Trauma Bonds in Co-Parenting

You may find yourself replaying interactions, second-guessing decisions, or feeling exhausted by emotional vigilance. The cycle is exhausting because it's wired into the biology of attachment—your body responds to cues of safety and danger long before your conscious mind can catch up. Anthropologically, humans are designed to stay connected to those who influence survival and safety, which explains why leaving—even emotionally—isn't simple or instantaneous.

Healing in this context isn't about cutting ties or expecting perfect cooperation. It's about building your internal resources, strengthening boundaries, and learning to soothe your nervous system without depending on your co-parent for emotional regulation. It's about noticing the cycle, understanding the pulls and triggers, and reclaiming your agency. By doing so, you create space to parent from presence rather than reaction, to witness your child's bond without absorbing its chaos, and to honor your own emotional experience. Over time, you can disentangle your wellbeing from the unpredictable patterns of abuse, trusting that your capacity for empathy, patience, and resilience doesn't make you weak—it makes you both a protective anchor and a model of stability for your child.

In short, trauma bonds in co-parenting are a complex dance of attachment, hope, and survival. Recognizing the biology, psychology, and human instinct behind these bonds gives you permission to approach them with awareness, strategy, and compassion—for your child, for your co-parent, and, most importantly, for yourself. You are not failing by feeling pulled or conflicted; you are responding to a system designed to keep connection alive even in impossible circumstances.

What patterns do I notice in my emotional connection to my co-parent?

Describe cycles of hope, pain, relief, or confusion.

What patterns do I notice in my emotional connection to my co-parent?

How does the trauma bond affect my sense of self and decision-making?

Reflect on moments when the bond clouds your clarity.

How does the trauma bond affect my sense of self and decision-making?

What moments make me feel temporarily safe or hopeful in this co-parenting relationship?

Identify triggers of the bond's pull.

What moments make me feel temporarily safe or hopeful in this co-parenting relationship?

How do I experience the push-pull dynamic in my body and emotions?

Notice sensations or feelings tied to the bond.

How do I experience the push-pull dynamic in my body and emotions?

What internal resources do I already have to soothe myself when the bond pulls tight?

List your coping skills and supports.

What internal resources do I already have to soothe myself when the bond pulls tight?

How can I remind myself of my autonomy, even when I feel trapped?

Write affirmations or mantras that reinforce your freedom.

How can I remind myself of my autonomy, even when I feel trapped?

What boundaries help me disrupt the trauma bond cycle?

Identify limits that protect your emotional health.

What boundaries help me disrupt the trauma bond cycle?

How can I nurture my relationship with my child independent of the trauma bond?

Reflect on the love and connection that is yours alone.

How can I nurture my relationship with my child independent of the trauma bond?

TRACING THE TRUTH

MAPPING THE EMOTIONAL WEB

Trauma bonds in co-parenting are tangled, not just between you and your co-parent, but also between your child and the other parent. Seeing these connections visually can help you recognize patterns, clarify your role, and identify where you can create healthy boundaries and emotional space.

Why it helps:
By externalizing the relationships and the emotional pull, you can step back from the intensity, notice where you feel trapped, and begin practicing perspective and control without blame. This gives your nervous system permission to release some of the constant vigilance.

Examine the Circle Diagram:

Connect the circles with lines to represent relationships.
Label Emotional Pulls: On each connecting line, write the feelings that flow between those roles: love, fear, hope, frustration, guilt, or protection. Include both positive and stressful emotions.

Notice Patterns: Circle or highlight lines that feel most draining, confusing, or intense. These are the areas where trauma bonds are strongest.
Ask yourself: Where am I absorbing tension I don't need to? Where can I strengthen boundaries or emotional detachment without abandoning my child?

On the side of the page, write a paragraph describing what you notice: "I feel pulled toward my co-parent when I see my child disappointed... I notice I tighten up, replay conversations, and feel exhausted..."

TRACING THE TRUTH

MAPPING THE EMOTIONAL WEB

My Child

Me

My Co-Parent

CHECKPOINT

The Trauma Bond Pull

Trauma bonding is a powerful, deeply ingrained cycle — slipping back is part of the journey, not failure. If you find yourself drawn in despite your intentions, pause without shame. Use your grounding and visualization tools. Reach out for support if needed. Remember, healing is a process, not a straight line.

Letters To Your Future Self

Write a letter from your future self who has broken free from the trauma bond's pull. What encouragement do they offer about reclaiming your peace and power?

Letters To Your Future Self

SHELF IT FOR LATER

Sometimes intrusive images or thoughts crash in like uninvited guests — too loud, too vivid, too much. Trying to "not think about it" only makes them louder. Containment gives your mind a safe boundary. Instead of battling the thoughts, you acknowledge them, then choose to store them somewhere secure until you're resourced enough to revisit them (ideally with therapeutic support). This isn't avoidance — it's wise pacing. By practicing containment, you send a message to your nervous system that you're in charge of when and how you engage. It builds trust with yourself, lowers overwhelm, and allows you to get through the present moment without drowning in unfinished business.

Visualize a container
Pick something sturdy — a jar, vault, chest, box, or even a digital safe.

Name the intrusion
Briefly identify the image, memory, or thought you want to contain. Write it in this jar here.

Place it inside
Imagine physically setting it in the container.

Seal it shut
Hear the latch click, see the lock turn, or feel the heaviness of the lid close.

Store it away
Place the container on a high shelf, deep cave, or secure room in your mind.

Return only with support
Remind yourself you can revisit it later with a therapist, journal, or trusted guide.

LESSONS IN INK

After hardship, the brain often circles around the why — why it happened, why you stayed, why you're still hurting. Meaning-making is a way to gently reclaim authorship. By naming what you survived and drawing out what it taught you about your own values and limits, you shift from being swallowed by the story to becoming the narrator of it. This process isn't about silver linings or forced positivity. It's about grounding your pain in context — saying, this mattered, this shaped me, and here's what I'm carrying forward. Closing with a boundary sets a line in the sand: you're not just reflecting on what happened, you're deciding how it changes the way you'll protect yourself in the future.

Headline: Write a short, bold line that sums up what you survived (as if it were on the front page of your personal newspaper).

Lessons: List 3–5 things it revealed about your needs, your limits, or your values.

Boundary: Write one clear, non-negotiable boundary you'll honor from now on.

SECTION NINE

Self-Forgiveness & Untangling the Shame Spiral

When you're co-parenting with an emotional abuser, it's all too easy to get caught in a relentless shame spiral — that heavy, grinding feeling that you're somehow failing, not enough, or responsible for things outside your control. Shame is a shadow that can seep into every thought, making self-forgiveness feel impossible. Yet, healing depends on breaking free from this exhausting loop.

In this section, we'll gently untangle shame's grip and create space for self-forgiveness — not as a one-time act, but a daily practice that honors your humanity. You'll learn how shame and guilt differ, why forgiveness doesn't mean excusing abuse or forgetting boundaries, and how offering yourself kindness is the most radical, courageous step you can take. This is about reclaiming your worth and stepping out of self-judgment so you can parent and live with greater peace.

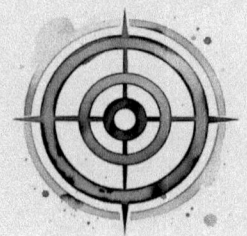 Trigger Check-In

After a heated exchange, you replay the conversation repeatedly, telling yourself, "I shouldn't have said that. I'm a bad parent." The shame spirals, weighing heavily in your chest. Instead of sinking deeper, you pause, breathe, and remind yourself: "I'm doing the best I can in a difficult situation." You begin to write a forgiving letter to yourself.

I see how hard it is to carry shame like a stone in your heart. I see the battles you fight inside, the nights of doubt and self-criticism. You are not alone. Your efforts matter, your feelings are valid, and forgiveness is a gift you deserve — especially from yourself.

Making Sense Of It
Shame, Self-Forgiveness, and Reclaiming Your Inner Authority

Shame is a silent predator. It thrives in isolation, secrecy, and harsh self-judgment, whispering that your mistakes or struggles define your worth. When co-parenting with someone who is emotionally abusive, shame is amplified: the abuser projects blame, manipulates perception, and distorts reality, leaving you carrying weight that is not yours to bear. Unlike guilt, which points to something specific you did or didn't do, shame attacks the very core of your identity, convincing you that there is something inherently wrong with who you are. It makes you question whether you are a "good parent," a capable adult, or even a lovable human being.

Self-forgiveness is not a shortcut or a way to dismiss the reality of abuse. It doesn't excuse harmful behavior, nor does it blur the boundaries you need to protect yourself and your child. Instead, it is an intentional, radical act of compassion toward yourself. It acknowledges that you are human, navigating impossible circumstances, doing the best you can with the tools and energy you have. By practicing self-forgiveness, you begin to reclaim authority over your emotional experience rather than surrendering it to internalized criticism or external manipulation.

Making Sense Of It
Shame, Self-Forgiveness, and Reclaiming Your Inner Authority

Neuroscience shows that trauma and repeated criticism can hardwire your nervous system to default to shame, keeping you in cycles of self-doubt and hypervigilance. Every act of self-compassion, every moment you tell yourself the truth about your efforts and limits, rewires these pathways. You strengthen your resilience, restore a sense of self-worth, and open space for clarity, confidence, and emotionally grounded parenting. In essence, self-forgiveness transforms shame from a cage into a bridge—one that allows you to move forward, protect your child, and parent from a place of authenticity rather than fear.

Shame will likely return, especially in moments of conflict, isolation, or projection from your co-parent—but each time you meet it with honesty and self-compassion, you chip away at its power. You are not broken. You are not inherently flawed. You are learning, surviving, and growing in a landscape designed to challenge your boundaries and your sense of self. Self-forgiveness is your tool to navigate that terrain with courage, steadiness, and love for yourself.

# What are the recurring shame messages I tell myself related to co-parenting?

Identify the harshest inner criticisms.

What are the recurring shame messages I tell myself related to co-parenting?

How does shame affect my behavior and choices with my co-parent?

Explore how shame influences your interactions.

How does shame affect my behavior and choices with my co-parent?

What distinctions can I draw between guilt (feeling responsible for actions) and shame (feeling flawed)?

Reflect on how these emotions show up differently.

What distinctions can I draw between guilt (feeling responsible for actions) and shame (feeling flawed)?

When have I practiced self-forgiveness, even in small ways?

Recall moments of kindness toward yourself.

When have I practiced self-forgiveness, even in small ways?

What beliefs about forgiveness might be keeping me stuck?

Challenge ideas that forgiveness means weakness or forgetting.

What beliefs about forgiveness might be keeping me stuck?

How can I create a self-forgiveness ritual or practice?

Brainstorm rituals that nurture healing.

How can I create a self-forgiveness ritual or practice?

What boundaries can I maintain that support my self-worth?

List limits that protect you emotionally and physically.

What boundaries can I maintain that support my self-worth?

How can self-forgiveness help me model healthier emotional patterns for my child?

Reflect on the legacy of compassion you want to build.

How can self-forgiveness help me model healthier emotional patterns for my child?

TRACING THE TRUTH

LETTERS TO SHAME AND TO YOURSELF

Shame often speaks the loudest when no one else is listening. This exercise gives that voice a space to be heard—but also allows your own voice of compassion and truth to answer it. By separating the two, you reclaim control and begin rewiring old patterns of self-judgment.

Why it helps:
Naming shame and responding from a compassionate perspective strengthens your nervous system, reduces internalized blame, and builds self-trust. It transforms shame from a silent saboteur into a teacher you can listen to without being controlled by it.

Write a letter from Shame to You
Name the voice of shame—Is it harsh, critical, disappointed?
Let it speak freely: all the "You failed," "You're not enough," or "You shouldn't feel this" statements. Don't censor or edit.

Write a letter from Your Compassionate Self
Respond as the part of you that sees the bigger picture.
Include acknowledgment: "I see how hard this is. You did the best you could."
Include reassurance: "Making mistakes doesn't make you unworthy. You are learning, surviving, and protecting what matters."

TRACING THE TRUTH

LETTERS TO SHAME AND TO YOURSELF

TRACING THE TRUTH

LETTERS TO SHAME AND TO YOURSELF

TRACING THE TRUTH

LETTERS TO SHAME AND TO YOURSELF

TRACING THE TRUTH

LETTERS TO SHAME AND TO YOURSELF

CHECKPOINT

Shame Creeping In

Shame can return unexpectedly, especially after conflict or perceived mistakes. When this happens, remember relapse is part of healing, not failure. Use your affirmations, breathwork, and somatic exercises to ground yourself. Reach out for support if needed, and remind yourself that self-forgiveness is a practice — a daily choice, not a destination.

SAFETY IN SENSATION

After stress, trauma, or relational upheaval, our bodies often feel like a battleground—tense, guarded, or disconnected. Reclaiming the body is about coming back home to yourself. By practicing gentle, nurturing touch, you signal to your nervous system that it's safe to soften. This isn't indulgence; it's essential care. Daily attention to your physical self strengthens body awareness, lowers chronic tension, and reminds you that your body is a safe place, not just a vessel for pain. Over time, these small acts become proof: I can care for myself, and my body can be trusted again.

1 PICK A NURTURING TOUCH
Examples include rubbing lotion into your hands, sinking into a warm bath, wearing soft or comforting clothes, or even a gentle hand on your chest.

2 ENGAGE FULLY
Notice textures, warmth, weight, or scents — bring mindful awareness to the sensation.

3 BREATHE INTO THE TOUCH
Let each inhale gather calm, each exhale release tension.

4 PRACTICE DAILY
Even 2–5 minutes consistently signals safety and care.

5 NOTICE CHANGES
Check in with your body and note any softening, release, or increased comfort over time.

WORRY WINDOW

Worries often hijack your mind, showing up at every unexpected moment. By giving them a dedicated "time slot," you reclaim control instead of letting them run your day. This practice teaches your nervous system that there's a safe space and a safe time to process, so you're not constantly reacting to every intrusive thought. During the window, you can gently evaluate what's actionable versus what you need to let go, building clarity and self-trust. Outside the window, a simple cue like "not now—later" helps you return to the present without guilt or shame. Over time, this simple structure reduces the intensity and frequency of anxious loops.

Park your worries: Write them down as they arise.

....

....

....

....

Set a 15-minute window: Choose a consistent time each day for processing.

....

Outside the window: Use a cue phrase like "not now—later" to return to your day.

Inside the window: Review the list. Solve what's actionable, accept what isn't, and release judgment.

Close the window: End with a grounding or soothing activity to signal completion.

BRINGING IT ALL TOGETHER

Notice how the skills you're learning connect and build on each other. This is where your learning starts to feel real and whole.

HOW DOES AN EARLIER SKILL OR INSIGHT RELATE TO WHAT YOU'RE LEARNING NOW?

CAN YOU SPOT MOMENTS WHERE THESE TOOLS OVERLAP OR SUPPORT EACH OTHER?

HOW MIGHT COMBINING THEM CREATE STRONGER RESULTS?

SECTION TEN

Relearning Love — What Healthy Relationships Actually Feel Like

After enduring the emotional turbulence of co-parenting with an abuser, the idea of what "love" looks and feels like can become blurred, distorted, or even lost. You might find yourself doubting whether healthy love exists or feeling unsure how it shows up in everyday life. This section is about relearning love — reclaiming your sense of what a safe, nurturing, and respectful relationship truly feels like, both with others and within yourself.

You'll explore how healthy love contrasts with patterns of abuse and control, and discover the emotional and somatic cues that signal safety, connection, and mutual respect. These insights will help you identify and nurture loving dynamics — with your child, your co-parent where possible, and most importantly, within your own heart. This is about rebuilding trust in love itself, so you can move forward with hope, clarity, and healthy boundaries.

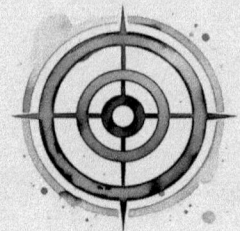 Trigger Check-In

> You notice a rare moment where your co-parent calmly listens without interrupting during a conversation about your child's schedule. Your body feels a small, unfamiliar ease. You recognize this as a glimpse of healthy connection, and you take note — this is what respect and cooperation can feel like, even if it's rare.

> I see the yearning in your heart to experience love that feels safe and real. I see the confusion and mistrust that come from past hurt. You're learning new ways to feel and recognize love, and that takes courage. Your capacity to love and be loved is not lost — it's waiting to be reclaimed gently and on your terms.

Making Sense Of It
Relearning What Safe Love Feels Like

Healthy love is more than an abstract idea—it's a felt experience in the body. It activates the nervous system's safety pathways, bringing a sense of ease, warmth, and connection rather than hypervigilance or tension. Unlike trauma bonds, which spike adrenaline and keep us on edge, safe relationships provide steadiness, predictability, and reciprocity. This safety isn't just comforting—it allows trust, openness, and authentic communication to grow. When the body feels safe, vulnerability becomes possible without fear of exploitation or shame.

Relearning love after trauma means noticing how your body responds to connection. A softening in the chest, slower breathing, ease in posture—these are your nervous system signaling that you are truly safe. It's also about observing relational patterns: respect, consistency, and kindness aren't occasional perks—they are foundational. This awareness equips you to make conscious choices about who deserves your time, energy, and emotional investment, including in co-parenting dynamics where interactions may remain complicated.

This process takes patience and repeated practice. Abuse can leave the nervous system wired to anticipate danger, and trauma can distort what "love" looks or feels like. But with each moment you allow yourself to receive care safely, recognize healthy patterns, and maintain boundaries, you are retraining your body and mind to expect safety instead of chaos. Over time, these small, steady experiences rebuild your capacity to give and receive love in ways that honor your worth, your needs, and your resilience.

What feelings or sensations arise in my body when I experience safety and respect?

Tune into subtle emotional and physical cues.

What feelings or sensations arise in my body when I experience safety and respect?

How does healthy love differ from what I experienced in the past?

Contrast feelings and behaviors.

How does healthy love differ from what I experienced in the past?

What boundaries help me feel safe and respected in relationships?

Identify non-negotiables for your wellbeing.

What boundaries help me feel safe and respected in relationships?

How can I nurture love and connection with my child in ways that feel healthy?

Reflect on your parenting goals and values.

How can I nurture love and connection with my child in ways that feel healthy?

When have I experienced kindness, consistency, or respect from others recently?

Recall positive interactions to reinforce hope.

When have I experienced kindness, consistency, or respect from others recently?

What internal messages do I want to cultivate about love and worthiness?

Write affirmations or compassionate truths.

What internal messages do I want to cultivate about love and worthiness?

How can I practice self-love and self-compassion daily?

Brainstorm small, nourishing habits.

How can I practice self-love and self-compassion daily?

What does a healthy co-parenting relationship look like for me, realistically?

Visualize your hopes and boundaries.

What does a healthy co-parenting relationship look like for me, realistically?

CHECKPOINT

Old Patterns

It's normal to slip back into old patterns or doubts about love and safety. When that happens, gently remind yourself that relearning love is a process, not perfection. Use your mindfulness, meditation, and boundary-setting tools to stay grounded and connected to your healing path.

GENTLE BREATH FOCUS

When anxiety spikes, the mind and body race together — thoughts accelerate, heart rate climbs, muscles tighten. Counting your breath gives both something steady to follow. By pairing inhale and exhale with numbers, you create a gentle anchor that slows the nervous system, refocuses attention, and interrupts spiraling thoughts. This isn't about perfection or achieving ten — it's about returning to the rhythm whenever distraction occurs. Even a few minutes daily strengthens your capacity to notice tension, settle your body, and move through anxious moments with less overwhelm.

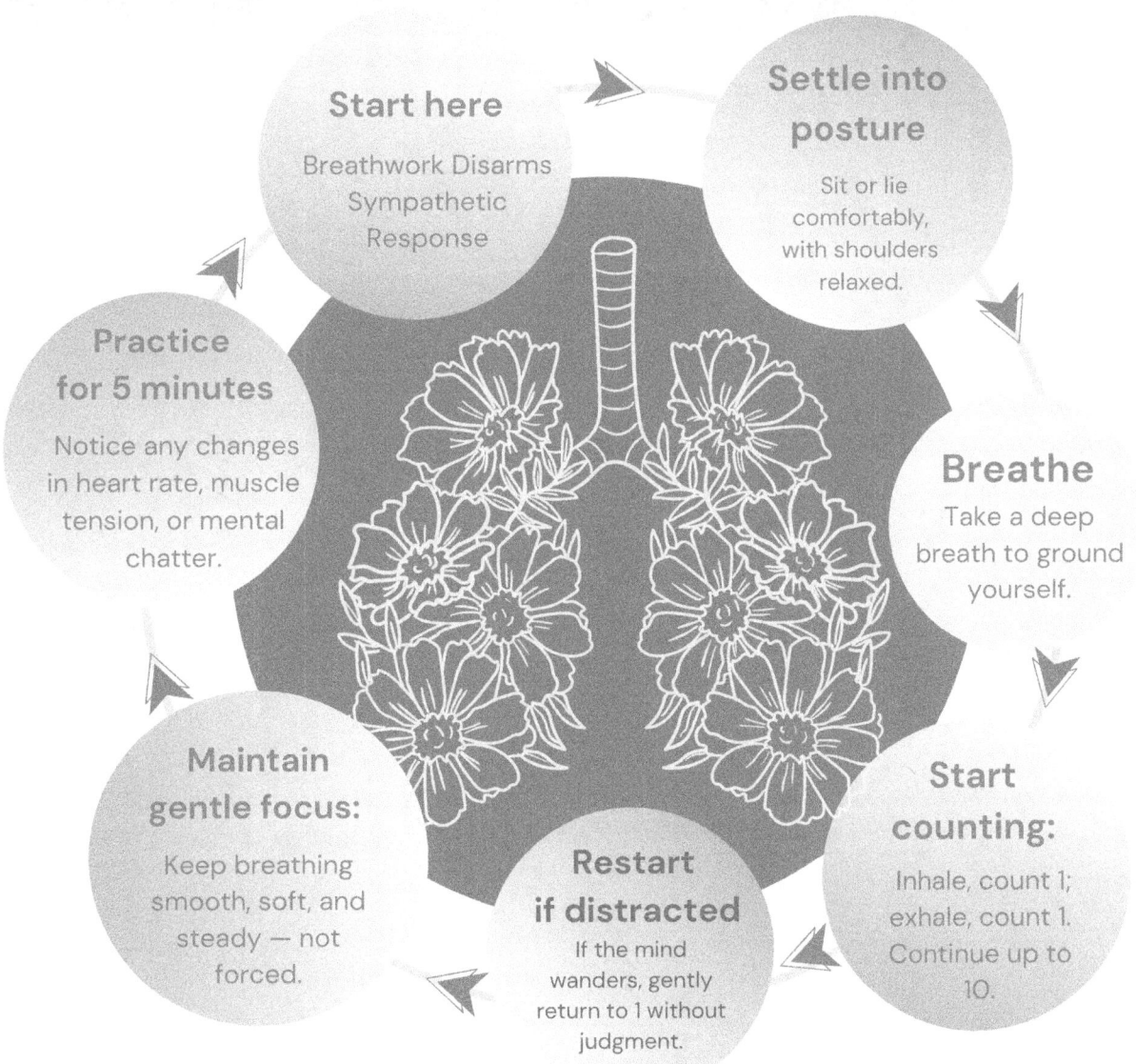

FEAR SCALE

Anxiety loves to inflate danger — suddenly a minor stressor feels like the end of the world. The Catastrophe Scale helps you step back and see the actual size of the threat. By putting a number on it and comparing it to your personal "0–100" life scale, you can measure proportion instead of panic. This clarifies what truly deserves energy and what doesn't, allowing your nervous system to respond appropriately rather than overreact. Over time, practicing this recalibration reduces automatic catastrophizing and builds confidence in your ability to face fears without being hijacked by them.

Identify the feared event and imagine it fully.

Rate it: Place it on a 0–100 scale where 0 is no impact and 100 is a true catastrophe.

Check extremes: Ask yourself, "What would a 90 look like? A 10?" to anchor your scale.

Place the fear: Decide the most accurate number for this specific event.

Choose a proportionate response: Match your actions and energy to the real size of the event.

Letters To Your Future Self

Write a letter from your future self who experiences healthy, nurturing love. What wisdom do they share about trusting yourself and others again?

Letters To Your Future Self

Letters To Your Future Self

SECTION ELEVEN

Future You — Trusting Yourself Again

Co-parenting with someone who has harmed you is exhausting in ways most people can't fathom. But here's the truth — you're not just parenting in the present; you're shaping the future your child will grow into. This section is about creating a vision you can be proud of, even when the other parent continues to be unpredictable, unkind, or unsafe. It's about learning to anchor yourself in your own values so you stop reacting to their chaos and start building something consistent, safe, and nourishing for your child. That doesn't mean you'll be perfect — far from it. It means you'll be intentional. You'll know what you stand for, how you'll handle the storms, and how you'll protect your peace while raising a child who knows what stability feels like. This isn't just survival anymore — it's conscious parenting in the middle of an imperfect reality.

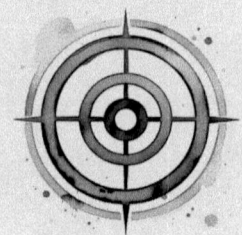 Trigger Check-In

You're at your child's school concert. Your co-parent makes a snide comment about the outfit you chose for your child. You feel the flush of embarrassment rising, and for a split second, you want to apologize just to make it stop. Instead, you take a slow breath, remind yourself that your child feels comfortable and happy, and choose not to bite the bait. You offer a polite nod, then turn your focus back to the stage. Later, your child beams at you and says, "I liked what I wore." That's the moment you know you made the right call.

I see the way you second-guess yourself after every small interaction, wondering if you've done enough to "prove" you're a good parent. I see the exhaustion of managing both your own emotions and the ripple effect of your co-parent's words. You are not overreacting. You are navigating a minefield with grace. Your parenting voice may have been doubted before — but it is still yours. It's still strong. And it's worth trusting.

Making Sense Of It
The Power Of One Steady Anchor

Children don't need perfection—they need presence, predictability, and emotional attunement. Even when the other parent's environment is chaotic, neglectful, or abusive, your consistent, grounded presence functions like a lighthouse in a storm: steady, reliable, and reassuring. This isn't about controlling what happens elsewhere; it's about creating a safe emotional home within your sphere of influence, where your child can feel seen, heard, and understood.

Resilience develops when children are allowed to express themselves honestly without fear of judgment or retaliation. Naming feelings, even difficult or uncomfortable ones, and meeting them with validation teaches your child that emotions are neither dangerous nor shameful. This is especially important when loyalty binds arise—when children feel pressured to protect or side with the unhealthy parent. By acknowledging their experiences without forcing allegiance, you help them maintain their own emotional truth.

Modeling emotional regulation is equally critical. When your child witnesses you managing stress, setting boundaries, resolving conflict calmly, and recovering after setbacks, they internalize those skills.

Making Sense Of It
The Power Of One Steady Anchor

They learn that intense emotions don't have to lead to harm, that boundaries protect rather than punish, and that self-worth isn't dictated by someone else's mood or approval.

Research in developmental psychology underscores the power of a single emotionally attuned caregiver. Even in high-conflict or traumatic environments, a child with one safe, consistent adult can develop a strong foundation for emotional health, empathy, and relational competence. Your daily acts of care—your listening, patience, and emotional steadiness—aren't just about surviving today. They are the tools your child carries into adulthood, shaping a future where they know stability, love, and their own capacity to thrive.

Recall a moment when your co-parent dismissed your parenting choice.

How did you feel in your body and mind? What did you tell yourself afterward? Where did that story come from?

Recall a moment when your co-parent dismissed your parenting choice.

Describe a time you trusted your gut about your child — and were right.

What helped you act on that intuition? How did your child benefit from you standing firm?

Describe a time you trusted your gut about your child — and were right.

Write about a situation where you silenced yourself to avoid conflict.

What did you lose in that moment? If you could replay it, what would you say differently while still keeping the peace?

Write about a situation where you silenced yourself to avoid conflict.

Identify three areas of parenting where you feel the most confident.

How can you lean on these strengths when your co-parent tries to undermine you?

Identify three areas of parenting where you feel the most confident.

Explore a fear you have about making mistakes as a parent.

Where does this fear originate? How could self-compassion change your response to mistakes?

Explore a fear you have about making mistakes as a parent.

Write a letter to your future self as a parent five years from now.

What do you want them to remember about their power, patience, and purpose?

Write a letter to your future self as a parent five years from now.

Think of a recent parenting win.

How did you create that moment? What does it say about your instincts and abilities?

Think of a recent parenting win.

Describe how you want your child to remember your parenting.

What specific actions today will help build that memory in their mind tomorrow?

Describe how you want your child to remember your parenting.

CHECKPOINT

That Feeling That Never Leaves

Even after you've done months of work, you may hit days where your co-parent's behavior sends you right back into that familiar knot in your chest. This doesn't mean you've failed — it means you're still human, still healing, and still parenting in a complex situation.

If you find yourself stuck:
- Notice the trigger, not just the emotion. Was it their tone? A specific demand? The timing of their message? Naming the exact spark helps you regain clarity.
- Pause the interaction if possible. A simple, "I'll respond later" can prevent you from reacting in the heat of the moment.
- Anchor back into your parenting goal. What outcome do you want for your child in this moment? Let that be the compass.
- Repeat a grounding mantra. Examples: "I am not who I was in this relationship." or "I choose calm over chaos."
- Do one regulating act before re-engaging. A brisk walk, a hand-on-heart breath, or writing a draft reply you'll edit later can all help you re-enter with composure.

TRACING THE TRUTH

YOUR FUTURE SELF

Write a letter to the version of you who is thriving in co-parenting—calm, confident, and deeply aligned with your values. Imagine it's 5 years from now. You've navigated hard seasons. You've set boundaries without guilt. You've shown up for your child in ways you're proud of.

In your letter, tell your future self:
- What you're most proud of in the way you've handled co-parenting.
- How you stayed grounded even when your co-parent was difficult.
- The ways your child has flourished under your steady, loving presence.
- What your daily life feels like without the constant tension.
- The promises you're keeping to yourself, no matter what.

End the letter with one line that you can return to on the hardest days—your personal anchor sentence—reminding you who you are and why you chose this path.

TRACING THE TRUTH

YOUR FUTURE SELF

TRACING THE TRUTH

YOUR FUTURE SELF

TRACING THE TRUTH

YOUR FUTURE SELF

TRACING THE TRUTH

YOUR FUTURE SELF

TRACING THE TRUTH

YOUR FUTURE SELF

SAFETY SIGNAL

Our nervous system remembers associations. When you pair a small cue — like a scent, a phrase, or a touch — with calm, it becomes a signal your body can rely on during stressful moments. Over time, encountering the cue can help shift your body from high alert to safety, even when anxiety spikes. This is not magic; it's a gentle, learned shortcut that reminds your brain: I have resources. I can settle. Using this practice regularly strengthens self-regulation and gives you a portable tool for emotional stability.

Choose a cue

Examples include a lavender scent, a short phrase like "I am safe," or a hand on your heart.

Pair with calm

During a relaxed moment, breathe slowly while engaging the cue several times.

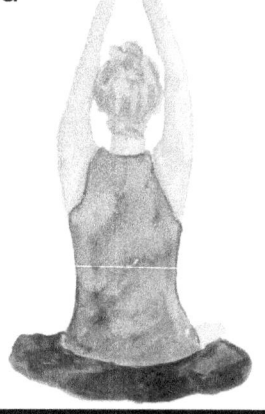

Practice

Repeat this pairing over days until your body notices the association.

Use during spikes

When anxiety rises, bring the cue into awareness while maintaining slow, steady breaths.

Reflect

Notice how your body responds and adjust the cue if needed.

TOUCHSTONE CALM

When anxiety spikes, the body often spirals into future fear or past memories. An anchor object works like a tether to the present moment. The steady texture in your hand gives your nervous system something solid and real to hold onto, cutting through the swirl of anxious thought. Touch is a direct pathway to calming the body — it grounds you without needing words. Over time, simply reaching for your object can become a learned cue of safety and regulation. It's a small, private ritual that says: I am here, I am steady, I am okay.

Choose your object: A smooth stone, piece of jewelry, or small token that feels grounding to touch.

Set intention: Decide: "This is my anchor. It helps me return to now."

Engage the senses: Rub or hold the object, paying attention to its weight, temperature, and texture.

Pair with breath: Inhale slowly, exhale fully as you feel the anchor in your hand.

Practice anywhere: Use during anxious moments, travel, or crowded spaces.

Reinforce: Each time you use it, the association between touch and calm strengthens.

STONEWELL HEALING PRESS

ASSESSMENT

HOW FAR I'VE COME

You've done the work — now let's see where you're at. Take a moment to rate these statements again with honesty and self-compassion. Notice what's shifted, what still feels raw, and what that means for your next steps.

1-10

1. I feel emotionally safe during exchanges or communication with my co-parent.

2. I can set and keep boundaries without guilt or second-guessing.

3. I trust my own perception of events, even when my co-parent denies or twists them.

4. I no longer feel responsible for managing my co-parent's emotions.

5. I can disengage from baiting or manipulation without losing my calm.

6. I have effective ways to regulate my body and mind after tense interactions.

7. I prioritize my own mental health and my child's well-being over pleasing my co-parent.

8. I believe I can create a stable, nurturing environment for my child despite my co-parent's behavior.

Mindset & Identity Shift Reflection

Healing changes the way you see yourself. You might notice you're less reactive in certain moments, more confident speaking up, or simply softer with yourself. This page is about spotting those shifts — the ones that show you're not the same person who started this journey.

In what ways do I see myself differently than when I started?

What beliefs about myself or others are shifting?

How has my sense of hope, strength, or trust evolved?

MOVING FORWARD

ACTION PLAN

This is your personalized roadmap for continuing growth beyond this workbook. Use this space to clarify which skills you'll keep practicing, how you'll notice early warning signs, and what concrete steps you'll take to support yourself. Remember, transformation happens one intentional step at a time.

Skills I will keep practicing regularly

Early warning signs or triggers I'll watch for:

When I notice these signs, here's what I will do:

MOVING FORWARD

ACTION PLAN

This is your personalized roadmap for continuing growth beyond this workbook. Use this space to clarify which skills you'll keep practicing, how you'll notice early warning signs, and what concrete steps you'll take to support yourself. Remember, transformation happens one intentional step at a time.

Ways I can check in with myself to monitor progress (daily, weekly, monthly):

People or supports I will reach out to if I need encouragement or accountability:

One commitment I'm making to myself right now:

RESOURCE LIST

The resources listed here are shared for informational purposes only. While they provide valuable support and tools for mental health, I am not endorsing or guaranteeing the quality, effectiveness, or availability of their services. It's important to explore these options and verify the details directly on their websites to ensure they align with your personal needs.

National Alliance on Mental Illness

www.nami.org

Offers free mental health education, peer support, and a 24/7 helpline.

Insight Timer

www.insighttimer.com

A free meditation app with thousands of guided meditations, music, and talks on mental well-being

Parenting for Mental Health

www.parentingformentalhealth.com

Offers resources, training, and advice on how parents can support their child's mental health, including guides and printable resources

Crisis Text Line

www.crisistextline.org

Offers free, 24/7 text-based support for mental health crises

7 Cups

www.7cups.com

Offers free, anonymous online chat with trained volunteers, as well as paid therapy with licensed professionals.

Healing is a long, painful journal. It's not pretty. It's not kind. It's brutal—opening wounds you can hardly bear to look at, naming truths you've avoided for years, facing the exhaustion of showing up again and again. And co-parenting with an emotional abuser? You don't get the luxury of walking away. You're stuck in the storm. There's no sunny escape. The chaos follows you into every conversation, every text, every bedtime, every heartbreak your child carries because of it. You've been living in the shadow of lies, where every day feels like walking on glass.

And yet—you're still here. You're still breathing through it, still trying to protect your child, still trying to keep yourself from breaking under the weight. That's not small. That is not weakness. That is proof of your stubborn, fierce love.

Some days you will rage. Some days you will cry. Some days you will wonder if it's worth it. And some days—if you're lucky—you will feel the smallest crack of clarity, a moment of quiet, a flicker of your own strength peeking through the storm. Hold on to that. Hold on to yourself. You are allowed to feel everything, and still be enough. Always.

> You can't keep running on empty. Small acts of care—like taking time to work through this workbook—are how you start to refill what's been drained.

M. Tourangeau
Stonewell Healing Press